The Professional Service of Food and Beverage

Joseph Houston
_____ and _____
Neil Glenesk

Batsford Academic and Educational Ltd   London

Typeset by Tek-Art Ltd, London
and printed in Great Britain by
Billing & Son Ltd
London, Guildford & Worcester
for the publishers
Batsford Academic and Educational Ltd
an imprint of B T Batsford Ltd
4 Fitzhardinge Street
London W1H 0AH

British Library Cataloguing in Publication Data

ISBN 0 7134 3529 1 (limp)

Acknowledgment

The authors and publishers thank:

Margaret Houston for research, reading and editing

Alison Glenesk for proof reading

J. Buchanan & Co.Ltd (Distillers) for providing the pictures and liquor used in the photographic illustrations

Ian Thompson, District Catering Manager, Western District, Greater Glasgow Health Board, for his co-operation in allowing facilities for photographic illustrations

A W Chisholm, OBE, Principal, Clydebank College, for the use of equipment

Joseph Devlin and A Y Herd for their excellent photography

The Authors

Joseph Houston MCFA
Mr Houston started his career in the thirties with British Transport Hotels and did his training in the company's leading establishments, "The Malmaison Restaurant" in the Central Hotel, Glasgow, Gleneagles and Turnberry Hotels.

After six years war service with the RAF as a Sergeant Instructor, he returned to the Central Hotel, Glasgow to resume and expand his career.

In the late forties he was asked to join the newly formed Scottish Hotel School at Ross hall and spent 20 years there as a lecturer in Food and Beverage Service.

During this time he provided assistance for Professor John Fuller's book, *Gueridon and Lamp Cookery* by compiling, preparing and partaking in photographic procedures, also at this time acting as Examiner and Assessor for The City and Guilds of London Institute and The Hotel and Catering Institute.

In the early seventies he spent four years at Napier College, Edinburgh, finally retiring from full-time teaching in 1976. Mr Houston can rightly be termed 'One of the Few' remaining pioneers of Formalised Scottish Catering Education.

Neil R. Glenesk Dip SHS MHCIMA MRSH DipAdEd
Mr Glenesk is a graduate of the Scottish Hotel School and has gained experience of the Hotel and Restaurant trade in both London and Sweden. He was formerly the Manager of The Grange Inn St. Andrews.

For a number of years he lectured in Food and Beverage Service at Kirkcaldy Technical College and Clydebank Technical College.

Throughout this time, Mr Glenesk has been extensively involved in the development of new education and training courses for the industry and has worked closely with both the Scottish Technical Education Council (SCOTEC) and SCOTBEC.

Currently, Mr Glenesk is Head of Department of Catering and Hotel Management at Clydebank College.

Preface

The aim and purpose of this book is primarily to provide a clear and concise up-to-date manual of the skills and techniques required by the new entrant to Food and Beverage Service.

The subject matter covered will meet the requirements of trainees and students who intend to take examinations in this field of study following courses offered by The City and Guilds of London Institute; The Technician Education Council (TEC); The Scottish Technical Education Council, (SCOTEC); or The Hotel, Catering and Institutional Management Association (HCIMA).

Instructors and Lecturers will find this text an invaluable reference.

Contents

Introduction

It was not always as easy as it is today to eat while travelling around the country. Travel belonged to certain sections of the community: the nobility, pilgrims, wandering minstrels, religious orders and the military. Most of the people never moved outside the confines of their own villages. The noble lords and ladies, travelled on horseback and were usually entertained by their own class in the castles and manors of great estates, they were fed and lodged, befitting their station, with gargantuan meals and gallons of wine. There was never any shortage of staff to prepare and serve these meals and no slacking. Guests' platters were kept well filled and wine flagons never allowed to empty. No one was off duty until the last guest had eaten and drunk their fill, and only then, were the retainers and serving men and women allowed the scraps from the tables.

The monasteries provided shelter for the religious orders and pilgrims, and soldiers never had any trouble in finding bed and board. It is fairly obvious that at some time an astute villager or farmer, saw the potential in providing, at a cost, lodgings for weary travellers. A warm welcome, a meal, a bed and a noggin of ale or wine, were basically all that were required.

The improvements in roads and the advent of carriages, made inn-keeping more profitable and more competitive.

Landlords improved their premises and comfort was established. Larger premises were built to acccommodate the ever increasing travelling public, and staff had to be trained in the finer points of food and beverage service.

The development of the railway brought an era of magnificient hotels at main railway stations. The elegance and grandeur of these establishments was epitomised in the excellence of their cuisine and the quality and standards of service provided.

Food and beverage personnel were subjected to rigorous training over a period of years before they could regard themselves as fully competent, but after such a training their own careers were assured. Changing travel patterns emerged with the motor car. It was now more convenient to stop at smaller less formal eating places and move on quickly.

Now air travel was becoming available and popular, providing cheap flights to hitherto undreamed of locations and taking from the railways and their hotels most of the business they once enjoyed. A new era had begun. Food was being served 'on the wing', high over the oceans and mountains, by smart young people skilled in the use of new technological inventions for preparing and serving food and drink quickly to large numbers of passengers.

Food and travel and people, an interesting mix which makes for a no less interesting career. The very nature of catering means involvement with people at a personal level, and the satisfaction of being part of a service industry which incorporates hospitality, leisure and tourism, important contributors to the economy of a country.

Those who are prepared to apply themselves, with diligence, to a course of study and training will acquire the knowledge and skills which will equip them for a satisfying and rewarding career.

1
Dining-room Brigade

Qualifications
To achieve the necessary standards, students require initially the desire to succeed in their chosen career, have initiative, a pleasant manner, enjoy meeting people and looking after them. They have also to be prepared to work unsociable hours, week-ends and public holidays.

Qualities
Most important are the three Ds: Discipline, Discretion and Diplomacy, these will be elaborated on later.

Appearance
Personal appearance is vitally important. First impressions are lasting. No potential customer expects to be met by a carelessly dressed individual with an unwelcoming attitude.

Reputations and future business can be put in jeopardy by the first personal contact between customers and members of staff.

Standards must be maintained at all levels.

Do not talk, argue or laugh loudly with colleagues in the presence of customers.

Personal hygiene
The close proximity between customer and staff which is necessary in the service of food and beverage, demands an extremely high awareness of personal hygiene.

Bad breath, body odour, dirty fingernails and long lank hair are totally unacceptable.

A bath or shower at least once a day, plus the use of a deodorant, is recommended.

Regular care and attention to teeth and the use of a dental mouth wash before going on duty ensures the removal of smoke and food odours which could offend guests.

Male staff should report for duty freshly shaved and wearing clean laundered linen.

Female staff must avoid the over abundance of clanking jewellery highly coloured nail varnish and laddered tights. make-up should be discreet and attractive.

Uniform

The wearing of uniform identifies your occupation, therefore its appearance can assist in giving a good impression of the establishment. It should be well-fitting and in good condition. The co-ordination of uniform with design and décor, along with other aspects, can help to create a harmonious atmosphere and give the guests a feeling of being welcome. Nothing should disturb or disrupt this impression.

Uniforms must be clean, well-pressed and kept in good repair. Missing buttons, tears in clothing and food stains should be dealt with as soon as possible.

Take a pride in your appearance, always look well groomed.

Great care must be taken of feet and footwear. A sensible approach to shoes is essential. They should be comfortable, low-heeled and of good quality, always kept in immaculate condition, clean and well polished. Regular visits to a chiropodist will prove to be money well spent. Heavily carpeted and tiled floors can play havoc with your feet and frequent changes of socks and tights are advised.

Attitude

Your approach to the customer should be friendly. Greet him with a smile, making him feel welcome, putting him at ease, attending to his needs, quietly, efficiently, and without fuss, showing courtesy at all times, even under extreme difficulty.

Treat the awkward customer as a challenge. This is where the three Ds — discipline, discretion and diplomacy — can be put into practice. Remember a smile instead of a scowl, plus a little tact and gentle persuasion, can placate an irate customer.

The old adage, 'The customer is always right' should be adopted more often today, with certain reservations, for without customers there is no business and, as a result, no job, so you have to look after your own interests as well as those of the establishment.

Aptitude

The skills required for the service of food and beverage at the table will depend upon the type of establishment, and all the various skills and types of service will be explained and illustrated in later chapters. The techniques and skills can be mastered with practice.

Personal qualities

Personality plays an important role in staff/customer relations, and can help to build and maintain a clientele.

Speech should be clear and as pleasant as possible, without affectation but avoiding the use of slang or coarse language. Familiarity should also be avoided, customers being addressed as 'Sir' or 'Madam', this is not demeaning, as some people imagine, but courtesy. Once the customers become known to you by name, by all means address them by it, because people enjoy being recognised and known, it boosts their ego, and gives them a feeling of importance. However, one word of warning, it is much more diplomatic to address the lady as 'Madam' at all times, thus preventing any embarrassment.

Memory is also a decided asset, remembering favourite tables and particular dishes that customers like.

Honesty must be strictly observed, as there are many temptations. Hence the need for discipline, for you will be handing food, beverages, and money.

Punctuality is a necessity for you are providing a service to the public. Make every effort to be on duty fifteen minutes before you are due, to enable you to check that everything is ready for service. Co-operation with colleagues is essential to ensure the smooth running of the establishment. Work as a team, this helps to create a pleasant atmosphere for the staff and, more important, customer, who is soon aware of any lack of harmony, and invariably suffering because of it.

Salesmanship is necessary to increase sales by presenting the menu and wine list in an attractive way, being knowledgeable of their contents. Food and beverage do not sell themselves, but need a little persuasion now and again.

Personal problems

Personal problems should be left at home and not discussed with customers, because they very often want to forget business or domestic worries when they dine out and are not interested in your problems. However, you sometimes are expected to lend a sympathetic ear to them.

This is where Discipline, Discretion and Diplomacy are put into practice, for whatever customers say, or whatever is overheard, in confidence, should be respected and not discussed with colleagues, the press, or even friends and relatives, for you are in a privileged position and should not abuse it.

The establishment's reputation and business could be affected if customer's affairs are discussed, business or otherwise, with all and sundry. Customers should feel relaxed in the establishment without having to be guarded in their remarks or conversations.

Organisation

The various qualities and qualifications have been pointed out. Now comes the preparation and planning of an organisation necessary to make a business viable and successful.

The restaurant organisation can best be shown by the personnel organisation chart on page 18, which will vary from one establishment to another. However there are a number of common principles which have to be considered first.

Dining-room Brigade

What is the purpose of organisation?
In food and beverage business there are so many different tasks and processes taking place simultaneously that a large number of people are necessary to carry them out. However, the aim of the operation is the same — that is to provide a service to the customer. It is therefore essential that everyone works towards that common goal. We organise the activities of different staff in such a way that the work is evenly shared out and the best abilities of staff are made use of. By having clearly defined jobs to do we can ensure that all members of staff know exactly what is expected of them and how their own work fits in with that of their colleagues. The added benefit of well organised work is that there is much less likelihood of an important task being missed out altogether.

How do we organise?
There is no one simple answer to this question, but there are a number of distinct areas to be covered and if we take the right steps in these areas we are on the right way to successfully being able to organise the work environment.

The first step is to define areas of responsibility
In this business although staff do require to be versatile there is still a need for employing specialists. Thus we define the different areas of responsibility in relation to the type of job, for instance, working with beverages should be a separate area from working with food preparation and the key person in each area will be able to concentrate on the knowledge and skills required for that particular activity. So, we have bar staff and wine waiting staff working together as a section of a larger team.

The second step is to define levels of responsibility
It is important that each worker knows to whom he is responsible, while one wants to avoid the, 'I'm in charge', attitude among employees, it is essential to indicate the various personnel who have a specific responsibility for the supervision of standards at different stages in the process.

A simple example of this would be where a commis waiter is required by his station waiter to clear away dirty dishes from the table or sideboard. The commis waiter would know how to carry out the task, but the standard to which he must perform is established by the more senior waiter who will state when it is to be done and how well it should be done. Not only will the staff member at that level of responsibility supervise the task but he will also have the responsibility to his own superior for ensuring that the work is done.

In fact we have a chain of command whereby each worker's accountability is closely linked with the authority expected to fulfil the requirements of that accountability.

The third step is to look at the patterns of interaction
It is very easy to set up a structure but much more difficult to get people to fit into the structure with willingness and without frustration. The best

14

way to develop a person's abilities is to fit a structure around their inherent qualities rather than restrain them in a straight-jacket organisation pattern, so we must now look at the patterns of interaction and the channels of communication.

If we draw an organisation chart it will show job titles and relative job positions but it does not show exactly what happens from these relative positions. To understand the practical everyday operation within an organisation we do not use pieces of paper, we use people, therefore the following key points are the ones that must be considered all the time in relation to any situation. A good employer will frequently ask himself these questions:

1 Is each member of staff being given enough responsibility?
2 Do people really understand the instructions that they are getting?
3 What is the best way to get someone to do something?
4 Are my employees satisfied with what they are doing?Can they do better?
5 Has the right job been given to the right employee?
6 Do the workers work as a team?

Interestingly enough, the employer will find it very difficult to get an answer to these types of questions for himself. He must consult his employees. He must communicate with them and understand their communications to him. Many a worker will not say directly how satisfied he is, but will readily express his dissatisfaction, similarly a supervisor must always remember the value of praise to a worker whose effort merits reward. What in effect one is referring to is the consultation between workers regardless of status. The organisation structure must not inhibit a free flow of ideas or exchange of opinions.

In a large catering establishment there is always the danger of the senior supervisors being extremely remote from the front line of operation and one can see from the various types of organisation chart which follow that as an operation increases in size it is best to divide the work areas into sub-sections or departments so that the work can be properly co-ordinated.

The restaurant area itself provides a natural division with the actual food service area and the beverage service area, both supported by a back-up of ancillary services.

Traditionally these have been the separate areas of organisation but one should always be prepared to examine a new situation and consider what is going to be the most effective way of organising the work.

The traditional restaurant brigade
The term brigade refers to the members of the staff who work in the restaurant or dining-room area, and the following list of positions details the duties and responsibilities which each of these people would undertake in a classical organisation. This type or organisation, however, is seldom found today, except in very large luxury hotels.

15

Dining-room Brigade

The restaurant manager — (Directeur du restaurant)

Responsible for organising, supervising, directing and administering the detailed routine work of the entire food and beverage operational areas.

This person would require to be highly knowledgeable in the business aspects and essential skills of food and beverage service. He would have full responsibility for the appointment and dismissal of staff and the training and induction of new staff. The evaluation of the needs of the operation and the efficient use of personnel would come within his responsibility. He would be required to maintain high standards of hygiene and sanitation in all areas of food service. Traditionally the restaurant manager would wear a morning suit during the day, and a dinner suit for evenings.

Headwaiter (Maître D'Hôtel)

This key figure would be responsible for the practical aspects of the restaurant or dining-room, assigning duties to other staff, he would supervise and co-ordinate the service staff to ensure the provision of an efficient service. In the absence of the restaurant manager he would be in overall charge.

His main duties would include the greeting of guests on arrival and conducting them to their table. The training of junior staff would also be his responsibility.

On a day-to-day basis the headwaiter would requisition supplies, compile and allocate duties and deal with customers. Such a person would require to be highly qualified in the techniques of restaurant organisation, staff control, food and beverage service and customer relations.

The traditional dress would be black tailcoat with black waistcoat and black bow tie during the day, changing to white waistcoat in the evening.

The less traditional dress, more common today is a black or coloured dinner jacket with bow tie, worn both morning and evening. It should be emphasised that there is considerable variation from one establishment to another.

Station headwaiter (Maître D'Hôtel de Carré)

Responsible for a section of the dining area comprising from eight to twelve tables, the station headwaiter would receive guests into his section and take their orders, assisting in the service where necessary, other duties are similar to those of the headwaiter for whom he might be required to deputise.

Traditional dress would be tailcoat, black waistcoat and bow tie at all times.

Wine waiter (Sommelier)

The wine waiter is responsible for the taking and executing of all orders for alcoholic and non-alcoholic beverages. Thus he requires to be thoroughly conversant with the licensing regulations for the establishment and needs to have an extensive knowledge of all aspects of wines and spirits in relation to their selection, handling and service.

He would be able to assist and advise guests in their choice of wine to accompany a particular menu item and generally promote the sale of beverages.

His day-to-day duties would include requisitioning and control of stock of beverages and the care and maintenance of glassware and wine service equipment.

Traditional dress would be black tailcoat, waistcoat and bow tie, with a grape design badge on the lapel or perhaps a chain worn around the neck to distinguish him from other food service staff. It is common, however, in the less traditional establishment to have the wine waiter dressed in a different coloured jacket from other dining-room staff, so that he can be easily identified.

Station waiter (Chef de rang)
To hold the position of station waiter one requires to be very highly skilled in the techniques of food service for the responsibility extends to the complete service of from four to six tables, including the presenting of menus, advising on and taking orders and carrying out the service smoothly and efficiently. Assistance is normally provided by a commis waiter but the main activities of service are his own responsibility and he should never leave his station unattended.

Traditional dress includes a tailcoat, black waistcoat and white bow tie worn both morning and evening. Whilst traditional dress has been retained by many establishments for their senior staff, it is perhaps the station waiter whose attire has been modified most, due to the problems of maintaining tailcoat used in a situation where a great deal of food handling takes place.

Junior station waiter (Demi chef de rang)
This waiter is not as experienced as his superior and will assist in the running of a large station, often by having the complete responsibility for one or two designated tables.

Traditional dress is similar to the station waiter with the white bow tie signifying his active role in service.

Assistant waiter (Commis de rang)
The term commis is commonly used in catering for both restaurant and kitchen staff to describe a very junior member of staff who is in effect serving his apprenticeship to acquire the skills of a full status position. The commis waiter who is assigned to a particular station will assist the waiter during service mainly by fetching and carrying from the kitchen and the ancilliary areas. He will probably help by serving vegetables and accompaniments leaving the complex service of main dishes to his senior.

Traditional dress is a black or white short jacket with black waistcoat, white bow tie and often a long white apron.

Assistant junior waiter (Commis debarasseur)
This is perhaps the most junior position in the traditional restaurant brigade and would be the first post to be taken by a young and

Organisation charts

The organisation of staff (Food production and service)

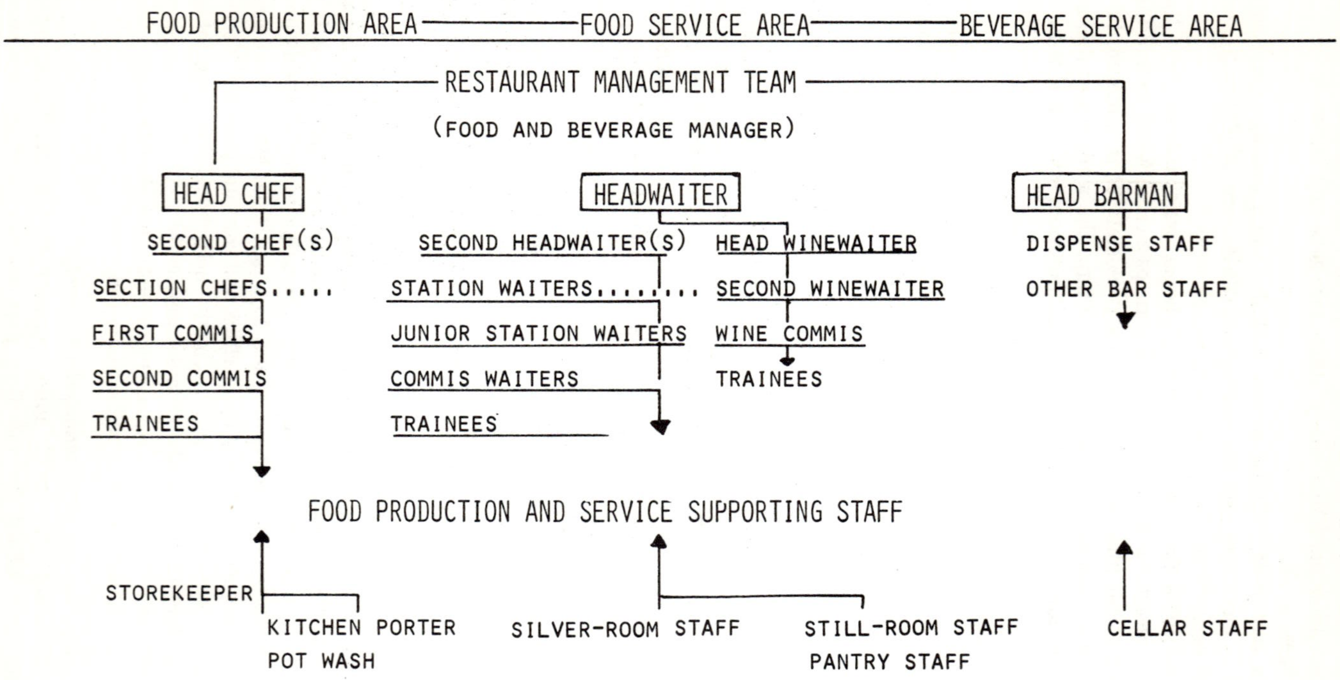
FOOD PRODUCTION AREA
FOOD SERVICE AREA
BEVERAGE SERVICE AREA
RESTAURANT MANAGEMENT TEAM
(FOOD AND BEVERAGE MANAGER)
HEAD CHEF
SECOND CHEF(S)
SECTION CHEFS.....
FIRST COMMIS
SECOND COMMIS
TRAINEES
HEADWAITER
SECOND HEADWAITER(S)
STATION WAITERS........
JUNIOR STATION WAITERS
COMMIS WAITERS
TRAINEES
HEAD WINEWAITER
SECOND WINEWAITER
WINE COMMIS
TRAINEES
HEAD BARMAN
DISPENSE STAFF
OTHER BAR STAFF
FOOD PRODUCTION AND SERVICE SUPPORTING STAFF
STOREKEEPER
KITCHEN PORTER
POT WASH
SILVER-ROOM STAFF
STILL-ROOM STAFF
PANTRY STAFF
CELLAR STAFF

The broad areas or responsibility into which staff can be organised

The traditional restaurant brigade

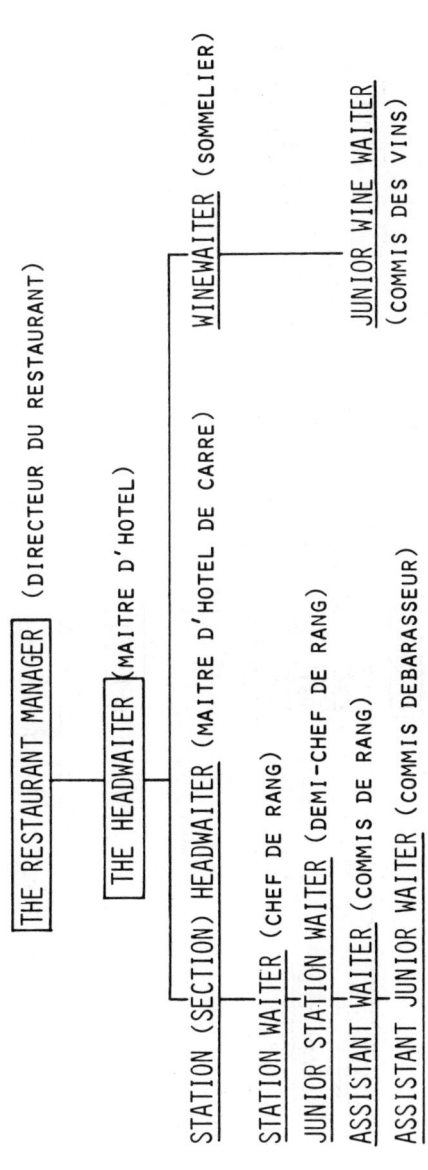

THE RESTAURANT MANAGER (DIRECTEUR DU RESTAURANT)

THE HEADWAITER (MAITRE D'HOTEL)

STATION (SECTION) HEADWAITER (MAITRE D'HOTEL DE CARRE)

STATION WAITER (CHEF DE RANG)

JUNIOR STATION WAITER (DEMI-CHEF DE RANG)

ASSISTANT WAITER (COMMIS DE RANG)

ASSISTANT JUNIOR WAITER (COMMIS DEBARASSEUR)

WINEWAITER (SOMMELIER)

JUNIOR WINE WAITER (COMMIS DES VINS)

The traditional hierarchy of dining-room staff with their French titles

The organisation of food production and food and beverage service staff for small establishments

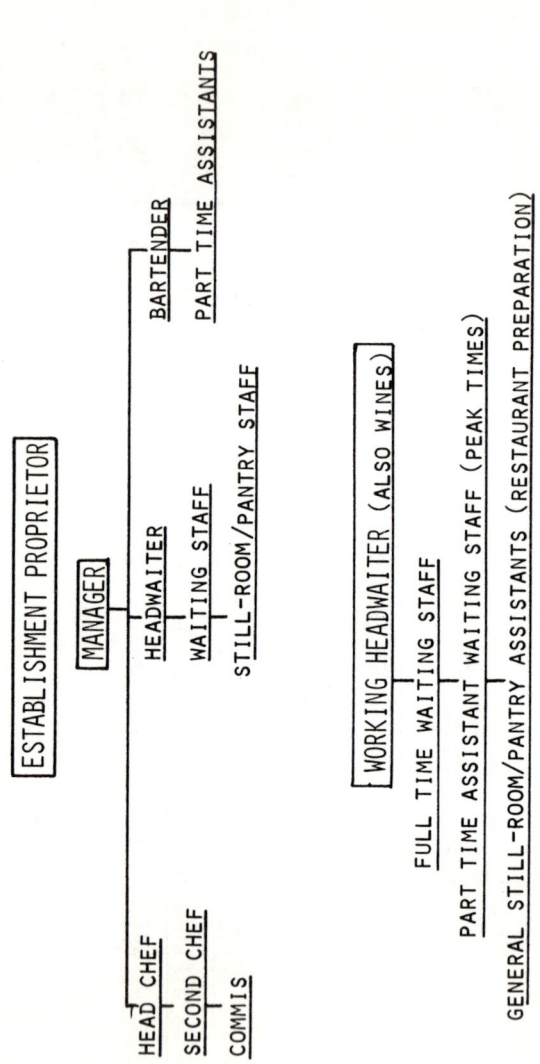

These two charts show how a small establishment can organise its few staff to cover the main work areas where a traditional brigade would be impractical

inexperienced person when they first begin their training. The main duties include the clearing of dirty dishes from the sideboard and the stocking of trolleys used in the service of hors d'oeuvres or sweets.

Traditional dress is a black or white short jacket, black waistcoat white bow tie and again often a long white apron worn during service.

Dress for food service staff

Considerable changes have been made to the traditional dress of food service staff which reflect not only the practical problems of maintaining uniform in a good state of repair and hygiene but also the different trend for fewer establishments to have a highly structured and totally male food service staff. Cotton or nylon jackets that can be laundered easily are used widely, and colour has become a useful feature when it is used to tone in with the décor or the establishments particular image. Uniform that is both smart and comfortable to wear and yet can be easily maintained is what is required for both male and female food service staff. Many establishments now provide the major part of a uniform for their permanent staff and it is only where a large number of casual staff are employed that the problem of uniform arises and there tends to be a resort to the traditional black and white, particularly in the case where these casual staff have to provide their own uniform.

QUESTIONS
1 What do you understand by the term, the three Ds?
2 How should you address a new customer when greeting them?
3 Whose personal problems may concern the waiter?
4 What are the three main steps in organisation?
5 What is a commis?

ACTIVITIES
1 Try to draw up a chart of your own establishment showing the different levels of responsibility within it.
2 List the personal qualities that make a good member of service staff.

2
Dining-room Equipment

Dining-room equipment represents considerable capital investment with today's high costs, and many factors have to be taken into consideration when purchasing furniture, glassware, crockery, silver and linen. The choice should be a combination of good taste, attractiveness, safety and hygiene. Everything should be able to withstand very frequent use and handling.

Versatility is an important feature to enable one to vary the dining-room, creating various themes and changes of atmosphere without further high capital investment. As many items as possible should be chosen that can have a variety of purposes.

First impressions are of great importance, therefore, the right choice of furnishings, fittings and equipment can contribute to the success of your operation.

Lighting also plays an important part in creating atmosphere, but has to be used properly. Avoid harsh white lighting, which is unflattering. Similarly, subdued lighting can be dangerous and a safety hazard if there is insufficient light for safe working. A variety of good lighting effects can be achieved with the use of colour, spotlighting and special effects. The atmosphere of the establishment can be greatly enhanced with the careful use of lighting effects.

When purchasing restaurant equipment there are a number of important considerations. The main points to be considered before making an investment in these items are:

1 the amount of capital available
2 the type of operation that is planned
3 overall design and décor
4 durability and flexibility of use
5 ease of care and maintenance
6 availability of replacements.

Tables

The sizes and shapes of tables will depend entirely upon the type of operation, type of service and availability of space.

There are three standard shapes, round, square and rectangular, however, most modern tables can be dismantled, folded, locked together and fitted to practically any shape you may require, with round top surfaces of varying sizes fitted on top of square tables.

Most systems are suitably flexible to alter the overall appearance of the room and accommodate different types of parties of special themes. A formal style of service requires more space with long or large tables, whilst the popular restaurant may have more tables to accommodate parties of four or six. An intimate restaurant would have a number of tables to accommodate two persons.

The top surface of tables can have a variety of finishes. If the tables are to be covered with cloths, then a felt, baize or heat resistant plastic foam can be used to deaden the noise of plates and cutlery, and to prevent the tablecloth slipping over the table.

Alternatively, composition tops of formica in various effects or colours can be used in a situation where guest turnover is high and tablecloths are not used. One might use such tables in cafes, snack bars, cafeterias or quick service restaurants where the table is merely wiped down between customers.

Table sizes

A round table for two should be 90 cm (36 in.) in diameter with a minimum of 75 cm (30 in.) in diameter.

A rectangular table for two should be 75 cm (30 in.) by 90 cm (36 in.) with a minimum size of 60 cm (24 in.) by 75 cm (30 in.)

A square table for four persons should be 105 cm (42 in.) by 105 cm (42 in.) with a minimum size of 90 cm (36 in.) by 90 cm (36 in.)

A rectangular table for four should be 90 cm (36 in.) by 120 cm (48 in.), with a minimum size of 75 cm (30 in.) by 105 cm (42 in.)

A round table for four should be 120 cm (48 in.) in diameter, with a minimum diameter of 105 cm (42 in.).

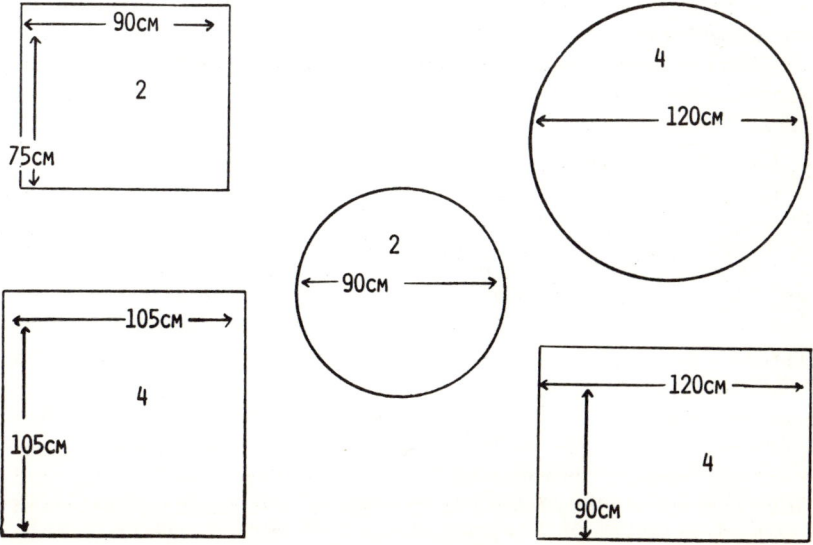

Table sizes (larger)

When considering the larger sizes of tables one has to bear in mind the comfort requirements for the guest with regard to adequate spacing and the avoidance of table legs. In fact the more modern design of tables with a centre pedestal type leg is suitable provided the feet are long enough to give stability.

A rectangular table for six should be 105 cm (42 in.) by 180 cm (72 in.) but 105 cm (42 in.) by 150 cm (60 in.) would be sufficient. When the ends of the table are not being used for seating, as is often the case in special table formations used at large gatherings, then the required size would be 210 cm (84 in.), or at least a minimum length of 180 cm (72 in.).

A round table would require 135 cm (54 in.) in diameter to seat six persons very comfortably, with 120 cm (48 in.) in diameter the minimum acceptable.

A rectangular table for eight would require to be 180 cm (72 in.) by 240 cm (96 in.) with end of table seating, but 270 cm (108 in.) long if not used at the ends for seating.

A round table for eight would seat very comfortably with 165 cm (66 in.) in diameter, but 150 cm (60 in.) would be sufficient.

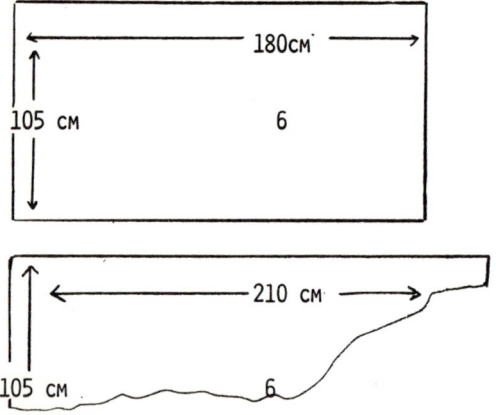

Table and chair dimensions

The top of the restaurant table is generally 75 cm (30 in.) from the floor and the seating should relate to this in order to position the guests correctly for comfortable eating and drinking. The seats of the chairs therefore should be about 46 cm (18½ in.) from the floor and about 45 cm (18 in.) wide.

Chairs with arms are usually wider and about 60 cm (24 in.), but it is important that they can be pushed under the table edge when not in use. When in use, a chair usually extends 40 cm (16 in.) from the edge of the table. This fact is important when planning room layouts, to have sufficient room for movement of guests and service staff. A chair back needs to be

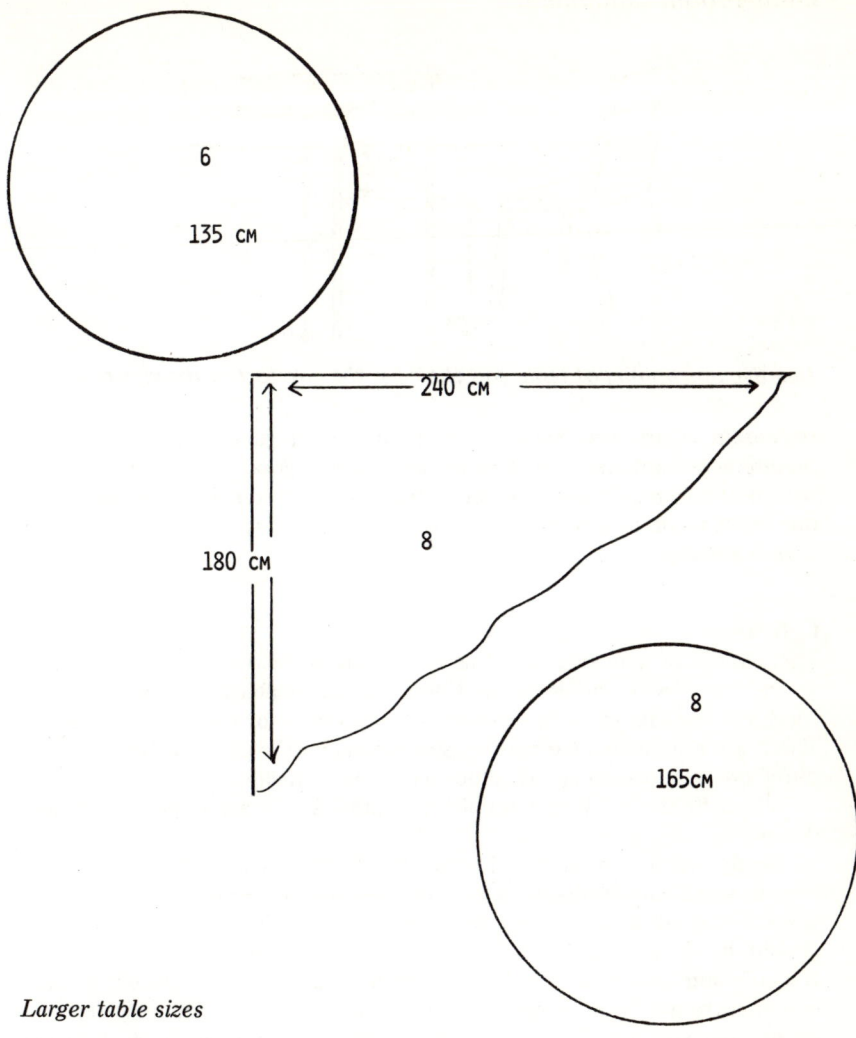

Larger table sizes

about 80 cm (32 in.) in length to give enough support without restricting the service activity.

The top of the seat lies at about 22-23 cm (9 in). from the underside of the table to enable the customers to sit comfortably without their knees catching on the underside of the table top. The height of the chair should be 42-43 cm (17 in.) and a good design should avoid a deep back or seat, or legs which protrude beyond the back, for these styles can be a safety hazard in a busy restaurant. The final chair covering or upholstery ought to be smooth and easily cleaned and fairly durable, as should be the whole structure of the chair, in particular the arms.

All too often one forgets that despite careful design and selection of

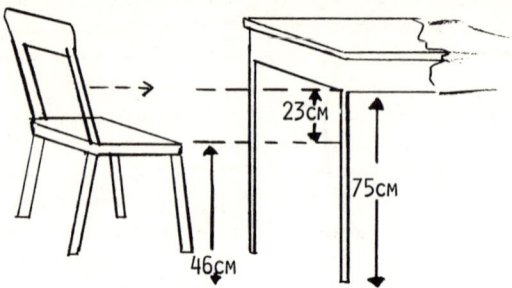

Relative positioning of table and chair for the comfort of the guest

restaurant chairs, provision should be made for guests who have special requirements not met by the standard chair, a good restaurant therefore will meet the requirements of both the irregularly dimensioned guest and the disabled or infirm guest. Special tabling and seating can be kept for such occasions.

Crockery

The choice of crockery for the restaurant is extremely important and should blend with the design and décor of the establishment, enhance the food and contribute to the customer's enjoyment of the meal experience. There are a number of major considerations with regard to the selection, purchase and stocking of crockery. These include paying particular attention to the quality, durability, suitability, storage requirements and design.

Firstly when considering the quality of the crockery item, one has to bear in mind that the demands of commericial enterprises are very different from those of a domestic environment, and a specialist manufacturer should be consulted. Considerable time and effort have gone into the research and development of these products, and to select merely an item of china from a store by personal taste would be folly. The manufacturer or supplier will be able to offer a range of different qualities at different prices from which to choose, in relation to other criteria.

Secondly one has to consider the wear and tear to which the crockery will be subject through constant usage, machine washing and possibly careless handling, in addition to high temperatures. If an item of crockery becomes chipped or cracked it has to be condemned at once to prevent contamination.

Above all one of the most important and difficult criteria to define is suitability, as there are so many aspects to this. Already we have mentioned the importance of design or pattern blending into the décor of the eating area. One must also be aware that this design should be sufficiently flexible to allow one to change the décor from time to time. A strong colour or pattern in crockery may create restrictions on the other décor.

A repeatable pattern is an important consideration, for unless one can carry very large stocks of spare crockery, there needs to be some form of guarantee from the supplier that, when required, the same style and pattern will be available.

A further consideration of suitability is the actual design and shape of some pieces. Different styles of food service operation and different menu ranges can require special shapes and sizes of crockery if the best presentation is to be achieved. Examples of this might include the presentation of a garnished steak being more aesthetic on an oval plate than on a round one. Similarly one may feel that an avocado pear is best presented in an avocado pear-styled dish. These are perhaps extreme examples, but the size of crockery is also extremely important in relation to other factors such as storage space, storage shelf design, tray size or even plate dispensing equipment.

One of the most common faults is to have too many different items of crockery that can be used only for one specific purpose. It is much more efficient to have a few different sizes that can be used for a very wide range of purposes. An example of this would be to have a small round tea plate of about 16 cm (6½ in.) in diameter, and use this not only for bread but also as a cheese plate, or an underplate for a sweet dish or coupe, instead of having as many as three different sizes of plate to serve each of these purposes. The size of the cup is important with regard to portion control if one considers the capacity as being an important factor related to the outage from a litre of tea or coffee, and the related cost. Whilst it is traditional practice to serve after dinner coffee in small half size cups or 'demi-tasse', the practicality of this ought to be reviewed in relation to the type of operation and the customers' requirements.

Storage of crockery is an extremely important consideration, not only because it is breakable, but the design has a great deal to do with the amount of space required when the items are stacked. If cups cannot be stacked one on top of another then shelf space is wasted. Similarly, if plates do not have a rolled edge then they can scratch one another when stored and moved about in large piles.

Whilst a reliable manufacturer or well-known supplier should ensure that these weaknesses have been ironed out at the design stage, one should beware of inferior brands which are cheaper but will not meet the requirements of a busy operation.

When considering the initial purchase of crockery one has to list the different types required, subject to availability these may be from the list of types that follows. The quantity should take into consideration the time for delivery of additional stock. The initial stock required will reflect the range of menu items, the speed of turnover of customers and the time required for the re-cycling of used items through the washing, rinsing and drying cycle. An approximate guide would be three times the restaurant's normal capacity of customers, although some items may require to be over this figure.

Finally, one could consider the merits of having a special pattern or badge or insignia on the crockery. This would make it more expensive of perhaps of greater souvenir value.

Range of crockery

Trade name	Main usage	Style	Approximate size
Side plate	Bread items Cheese Small savouries Underplate	Round	16 cm (6½ in.)
Entree plate	Hors d'oeuvres Fish dishes (single) Desserts Fruit Underplate	Round	22 cm (8½ in.)
Dinner plate	Main meals (complete)	Round	25 cm (10 in.)
Grill plate	Main meals Grill specialities Whole fish	Oval	30 cm (12 in.)
Soup plate	Soup	Round	23 cm (9 in.)
Soup bowl	Soups Cereals Desserts	Deep round	13 cm (5 in.)
Dessert plate	Desserts Cereals Soups	Deep round	15 cm (6 in.)
Teacup	Tea/Coffee	3 to a pint	5 to a litre
Demi-tasse	Coffee	6 to a pint	10 to a litre
Saucer	Underplate	To fit cup	
Specialist items	Cream jug or pot Milk jug Sugar basin Cruets Tea/coffee pots Egg cups etc.		

Manufacturers normally supply catalogues of their ranges of crockery including details of size, patterns and range of items available

Glassware

Provided the capital is available the correct glasses should be purchased, for it is said 'fine wine deserves fine glasses', and will contribute greatly to the general appearance of the tables and the room.

Many of the considerations which relate to crockery also relate to glassware. In fact the highest number of breakages tends to be in glassware, particularly when handled by inexperienced staff.

The particular glasses selected will depend upon the range of drinks offered and details of the styles available will be considered later with beverage service.

As with crockery the storage of glasses is an important consideration, particularly since very few types of glasses can be stacked.

A certain amount of wear and tear is experienced with washing, whether by machine or hand, and chipped glasses or cracked glasses must of course never be used.

Whether one stocks a large number of different shapes or a few basic but versatile sizes will again depend upon the availability of repeat patterns.

To maintain a glass stock, the handling of glasses should be properly taught and although glasses may be carried by hand with the stems placed between extended fingers and the bases flat against the hand, when guests are not present, it is important to master the skill of carrying glasses correctly loaded on a salver. When lifting glasses they should only be handled by the stem, so that the waiter's fingers do not touch the drinking bowl.

Silverware

The term flatware is more appropriate for table utensils as silver is not generally used today. Sterling silver is the most expensive type of item and used only in a very few establishments. 'Plate' or electro-plated nickel silver is much more commonly used to give the effect of silver. The life of silverware will depend very much on usage and the quality of the plate with the need for re-plating being anything from every five to every ten

years. Most common today, because of its hard wearing qualities, is stainless steel which, although not considered to be as attractive in appearance as silver, is available in a wide range of qualities and designs.

The quantity of silverware required for a restaurant will vary according to the type of menu offered, the style of service and the volume of business. Tableware items such as cutlery, cruets and coffee or teapots are required for most operations. The need for serving dishes will depend upon the style of service.

A good guide to the quantity of cutlery required is three times the restaurant's capacity, although one can manage with less. There will be certain items that are used much more frequently than others and some are required for service of food as well as for eating. To cover a normal full meal and provide the guest with a full table d'hôte setting the following are required: soup spoon; joint knife and fork; fish knife and fork; sweet spoon and fork; side knife; tea or coffee spoon.

Most manufacturers will provide details of the range of items that they can offer in any particular pattern.

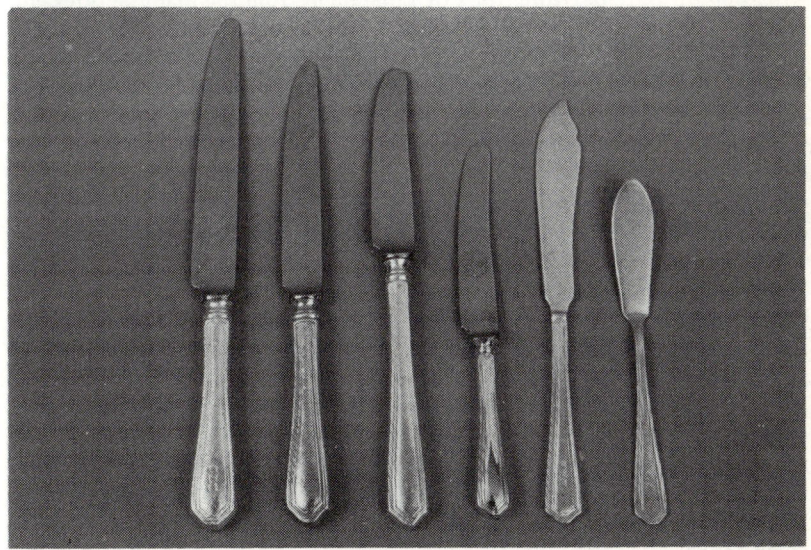

Linen

Linen is another expensive commodity, so the choice has to be taken with great care. There are many qualities and types, ranging from the finest irish linen to the synthetic materials now available.

Traditionally, formal dining-rooms and restaurants prefer to use white tablecloths and napkins, although the pastel shades are favoured in certain up-market places, and with themes becoming increasingly popular, various other colours are also being used.

Requirements again depend upon the size of the room and the turnover of customers. It also has to be considered whether the linen is to be processed on the premises or by an outside contractor. All linen stocks have to be kept carefully with usually a daily issue on the basis of one clean for one dirty, and a reserve stock to meet the requirements of special business and to cover the period of time required for the soiled linen to be laundered. It is usual to maintain about half of the total stock clean and ready for issue to meet the above conditions.

Table cloth sizes
The most basic sizes in use are as follows:

135 cm (54 in.) by 135 cm (54 in.) to fit tables 75 cm (30 in.) square, or a round table of 90 cm (36 in.) in diameter. This size allows an adequate drape over the sides of the table without interfering with the comfort of the guest when seated at the table.

180 cm (72 in.) by 180 cm (72 in.) would be the size for a table that measured 90 cm (36 in.) square.

180 cm (72 in.) by 240 cm (96 in.) is required for a rectangular table. It is feasible to purchase long rolls of table linen from the manufacturer and cut this to meet the needs of any special table lengths that are in use.

To protect the basic cloth on the table a slip cloth can be used to allow rapid changing and to extend the life of a slightly soiled cloth. These slip cloths should measure 90 cm (36 in.) by 90 cm (36 in.)

Napkins tend to be manufactured in a variety of sizes, some of which are too small to be practical at all. A good napkin needs to measure 45-50 cm (18/20 in.) square, with white being used for more formal occasions, but a variety of colours being available to blend with or contrast with the décor.

Paper napkins are often preferred for hygiene reasons, but these can vary greatly in quality and are seldom of much use if less than two-ply in thickness. The different cost has to be considered in relation to the quality and usefulness of the napkin.

Similarly it is possible to obtain paper tablecloths, usually in roll form so that the required lengths can be cut to fit any length of table. These tend to be used in popular restaurants where turnover is high and it is necessary to change the table cover frequently. Although some of these are in fact now washable, it is generally intended that they be disposed of when soiled.

A careful examination of the life and cost of linen compared with disposable products will help the restaurateur to make a choice in any particular situation.

Furnishings
Decorative features should not obstruct the service, but can be used to create a particular atmosphere or theme in a dining area. Whether a simple feature or very artificial environment is chosen one has to consider the maintenance, safety and practicality of the theme. With soft furnishings,

the colour and style should be one that is most versatile to allow for periodic change.

Ancillary departments

Service area
This is the area usually between the kitchen and the dining-room, where the still-room, wash-up, silver room and hotplate are situated. The area is normally the responsibility of the person in charge of the dining-room.

Still-room
This is where certain foods and beverages are dispensed, namely: hot and cold drinks such as tea or coffee, milk and fruit juices. If the operation provides a service for breakfast, afternoon teas and lounge service, then items dispensed would also include, toasted bread, scones, melba toast, brown bread, sandwiches, cakes, breakfast cereals and even porridge or eggs, etc.

To carry out these duties the necessary equipment would include: a refrigerator for the storage of butter, milk, cream, fruit-juices, etc. a still-set or hot water boiler unit capable of making tea and coffee and storing quantities of hot liquid. A steam injection unit is a useful addition. There are a number of portable coffee-making machines readily available which can be used, depending on the requirements of the establishment.

A large still-room area serving a number of outlets would require to have such additional equipment as: a bread-slicing machine, toaster, hot-cupboard, salamander, sink units, etc.

In a small establishment, it is not always easy to separate out the still-room area from the kitchen area, but the main function is the same.

Silver-room
This is the area where all the silver would be stored in suitable shelves, cupboards and drawers. Larger items would require large and very strong shelves to take the weight of dishes with a lockfast cupboard for all the smaller items, such as butter dishes, cruets, etc. Cutlery should be kept in lined sectioned drawers.

The main cleaning of silverware would be done in the silver-room usually on a rota basis, with regular daily cleaning for items that soil or tarnish readily. Stainless steel cutlery requires less regular cleaning and care, but if silver plated items are used then articles such as forks will require very frequent cleaning as the prongs tend to tarnish, particularly if they come in contact with certain foods.

There are various methods of cleaning, and cleaning materials available. For smaller items the technique of burnishing is ideally suited. A burnishing machine is a large rubber lined hexagonal drum which is half filled with ball-bearings, covered with hot water and plate powder added. The drum is sealed and when switched on it rotates slowly so that the action of the ball-bearings cleans the silver items gently without scratching.

Another method of cleaning silverware is to use polivit plate. Thin strips of aluminium sheet with holes are placed into boiling water with a little washing soda. The silver items are placed in this solution for only a few minutes and tarnish will be removed.

A commercial liquid silver dip is available for rapid cleaning, and articles only require to be dipped in for a few seconds. Slight tarnishing can be removed in this way, but articles must not be left in the solution for too long.

Plate powder can be used for larger items but is rather a messy method. Whatever method is used, it is important that items are thoroughly washed and rinsed afterwards before use.

Wash-up

It is important that this area is conveniently situated to enable a quick turnover of dirty plates, cutlery, crockery and glasses. Service staff have to play their part by stacking their dirty dishes in appropriate piles so that the wash-up staff can get them washed and returned for service more quickly.

Dish washing machines vary in size and are expensive items, but only a few small establishments still wash restaurant dishes by hand. The most effective type of dishwashing machine is one which feeds racks of dirty dishes in at one side and following the wash-rinse cycle, passes these racks of clean dishes out at the other side. This arrangement greatly speeds up the operation. Machines can be operated manually or automatically, with either hand fed detergent or automatic dispense. It is important that the dishes are properly washed and sterilised at sufficiently high temperatures to maintain a high standard of hygiene.

The layout of the dish washing area is important as it can greatly affect the flow of service to and from the restaurant.

Adequate shelves must be supplied for the storage of crockery and other items when not in use.

There should be suitable containers for the disposal of waste such as bones and paper items and a waste disposal machine for other waste food products. The person working in the wash-up area is generally responsible for maintaining an adequate supply of hot plates required for the service.

Hot plate

This is where the food is passed from kitchen to service staff, it should be properly stacked with the necessary plates for service and constantly replenished by the wash-up staff. Plate dispensing equipment can be used if there is limited space, or a mobile service is required.

Ancillary staff

Still-room, silver-room and wash-up staff are under the supervision of the headwaiter or restaurant manager in a large dining-room. A small establishment may only have one or two people who cover all of these jobs. Where there is a large staff they would work on a rota basis to cover the different meal times.

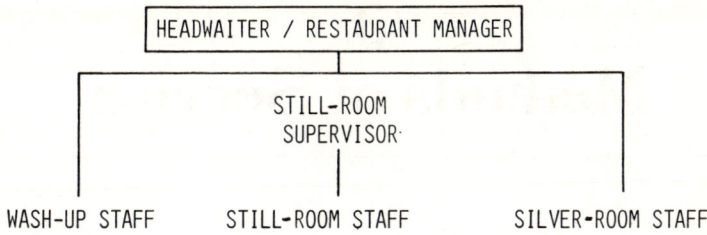

A still-room area in particular may have to be staffed for a twenty-four hour period if the establishment provides an extensive service. A large still-room staff might have its own person in charge of the team.

The main function of these areas and their staff is to provide a support to the dining-room staff and the service operation.

QUESTIONS

1 What are the main factors to consider before buying restaurant equipment?
2 Describe the relationship between chair and table
3 How much crockery should a restaurant stock?
4 What cutlery is provided in a table d'hôte setting?
5 What are the different ancillary departments?

ACTIVITIES

1 Select three different items of silverware and compare different cleaning methods.
2 Prepare a duty rota for a twenty-four hour still-room for one week.

3
Methods of Service

The evolution of service at the table
When eating habits became civilised and people found that there was a certain amount of pleasure to be gained from sitting and eating together, it became necessary for someone to serve them. This task was usually performed by servants or a member of the family or group. Gradually, by custom and habit, rules evolved around the complexities of the many courses, and eventually an ordered system became generally accepted.

Basic rules of table service
Serve all food from the left except when this is inconvenient for the customer.
Serve all beverages from the right.
The general practice is to clear from the right, but some establishments clear from the left.

All staff should follow the same rules for service and for clearing in order to give some consistency to the service.

Table settings
The term *cover* is used constantly in the hotel and catering industry, and it has two main meanings depending on the context in which it is being used.

The first one refers to the arrangement of crockery, cutlery, napkin and glass at each place setting on a table.

The second one refers to the number of people using the place settings. For example: the table has to be set with an à la carte cover for a booking of four covers (guests)

Another expression very commonly used is *mise-en-place*, which refers mainly to advance preparation.

À la carte cover
This setting is more frequently used in the luxury type restaurants and the minimum amount of cutlery is used for the initial setting, namely a fish knife and fork and a side knife, a cover plate, a side plate, glass, cruets, napkin and an ash tray.

An à la carte menu is usually very extensive and varied, and the food cooked to order. Each item is charged separately, therefore more expensive. The cutlery needed is determined by the guest's choice from the menu and is laid down on the table as required.

Table d'hôte cover
This setting is used in the more popular type of dining-rooms and restaurants, and the full range of cutlery is laid on the table: a soup spoon, joint knife and fork, fish knife and fork, sweet spoon and fork, a side knife on a side plate with a cover plate, napkin, glass, cruets and an ashtray.

A table d'hôte menu has a fixed price for the complete meal, which is generally already prepared, and any cutlery not required should be removed after the order has been taken and it is known what the guest has chosen.

These are the two main settings or covers, but there are many variations, for example: a function with a pre-arranged menu will have the cutlery laid out in the sequence in which the meal will be eaten, for convenience and to save time.

Principal methods of service
There are various types of service used today in dining-rooms, clubs and restaurants, which had their origin in the courts and large country homes of the European aristocracy, many of these are still in use, modified to suit modern requirements.

Each method of service generally retains most of its own features, however, any of the methods can be altered for particular needs. The main traditional forms of service are French, Russian and English.

À la carte table setting

Table d'hôte table setting

French service

This is a formal type of service requiring certain skills which can be attained with training and practice, mainly the manipulation of spoon and fork. The food, which has been prepared in the kitchen is served from large silver flats and dishes on to the customer's plate, endeavouring in the process to retain the original presentation of the food by carefully arranging it attractively and appetisingly.

The original French service differed from today's method. The food was brought from the kitchen on flats and serving dishes to the customer's table, presented to them, and they then served themselves. This is not practical today because of the importance of costs and portion control.

French service as we see it today is often referred to as silver service.

Advantages There is less chance of waste, because any food that is not served or required by the guest can be returned to the kitchen and utilised. Customers also get a more personal skilled service.

Disadvantages This method requires more skill and better trained staff. Much more service equipment is needed.

Russian service

This is a very personal service which demands considerable skill and training, as many of the courses are prepared and cooked in front of the customers at the guéridon (side table).

The food is then plated and placed in front of the customer at the table, complete, or the accompanying potatoes and vegetables can be served with a spoon and fork from the serving dishes.

Carving meat, boning fish, flambée-ing various dishes, all can be done at the guéridon.

Russian service is often referred to as guéridon service.

Advantages   Customers get individual attention. This service helps to promote sales and create atmosphere with the flickering lamps and tantalising aromas.

Disadvantages   The degree of skill required by staff is of the highest order. The operation is very time consuming and more staff as well as more elaborate equipment are required.

English service

This is a plated service which can vary according to establishments. The meals can be completely plated in the kitchen, or just the main part of the dish. Accompanying vegetables and potatoes may be left on the table in their dishes for the guests to serve themselves.

Advantage   Does not require very skilled or highly trained staff. Service is faster and equipment kept to a minimum.

Disadvantages   Standardised portions can result in wastage of uneaten food and a much less personal service with limited customer choice.

Buffet service

This type of service enables customers to select their meal from a variety of food attractively displayed on long tables. The customers either serve themselves or are served by chefs standing behind the buffet tables.

Service usually combines both types, with the main course being carved and served by the chefs, and the customers selecting and serving themselves with salads and vegetables.

The selection of food can consist of a complete meal with a choice of starters, main course of meat and fish with a selection of salads, and sweets.

There are numerous designs of buffets, the deciding factors would be the price charged, the numbers involved and the available space. The buffet can be either hot or cold provided that there is suitable equipment to keep hot food hot enough for service.

Plates, cutlery and napkins can be placed conveniently on the buffet table for the customers to pick up with their meal, or a cover can be set on the adjoining tables.

The main job at buffets for the food service staff will vary with the type of buffet and may be limited to the service of beverages and the clearing and setting of tables.

Advantage   The food can be attractively displayed. Service is much faster with a quick turnover of guests. Less service staff are required.

Disadvantage   A buffet can quickly lose its attraction if not kept re-plenished and fresh. The customer gets less personal attention than with table service.

Banquet service

This particular service refers mainly to functions or special business, for example: a wedding reception, conference, cocktail party, wine and cheese party, or dinner dance.

The actual service should not differ very much from the usual day-to-day operation, unless on certain occasions, a buffet or a special request from a customer.

Organisation and preparation are of paramount importance and timing is absolutely essential since everyone sits down to eat at the same time. However, numbers should be known and plans made accordingly, for food and beverage requirements, and the engaging of extra staff if necessary.

This is an excellent and lucrative type of business properly organised, which can operate separately, or in conjunction with normal business, depending on the size of the premises.

As this is a highly competitive market, functions, however good, do not sell themselves, and generally have to be advertised either via the media or by employing a sales person. Most of the larger hotel groups employ sales personnel to call on local firms, clubs and organisations who hold social events or business conferences, to promote the facilities of their establishment.

Organisation

A special function book must be kept for the initial bookings, with customer's name and address and telephone number. A record of the number of people and the date and time are also required.

When detailed confirmation has been received in writing this should be recorded in the function book to avoid the disastrous effect of double booking. Final numbers should be confirmed about twenty four hours before the function, and this would be the number charged. A special function file must also be kept with the appropriate forms giving relevant details of the requirements for each function: name, address, telephone number, date, time, number of covers, type of menu, and the charge per head. The wine and spirits to be charged to account, or cash bar, musician, group or disco, etc.

The department or individual members of staff involved should be notified by a memorandum containing the relevant information. In fact it is customary to issue a function sheet to all departments, a week or so ahead, this enables them to make up their duty rotas to ensure that the various functions will be catered for in every detail. The person responsible for function and special business must be in close liaison with all departments and staff concerned, and must check and double check, for there is little margin for error. Function business is staffed, even in the large hotels, mainly by part-time staff, with the permanent staff in the key positions.

It is advisable to have a pool of part-time staff to draw on whenever necessary. They are paid an hourly rate with a minimum of three hours, so that the hours of employment must be utilised properly to keep down costs.

There should be a variety of seating plans available for the customers to see enabling them to select a suitable one to meet their particular requirements, also a selection of menus and wine lists.

The menus should be interchangeable and the prices altered as necessary, avoiding, if possible a choice on their chosen menu, except perhaps of soup, or in special circumstances where one or two people are unable to take a specific dish, for particular reasons such as religion or vegetarianism, etc.

Apart from these possible exceptions there should not be a choice, otherwise service could be chaotic, causing a general dissatisfaction and complaints from guests.

Once the composition of the menu is known, the tables can be laid up accordingly, and the cutlery put down in the sequence in which the meal will be eaten. This allows the staff to have all the cutlery required on the table, saving valuable time during the service of the meal, for as stated previously, timing is all important. The staff are now free to concentrate on the service of food and beverage.

Service procedure

The allocation of covers served by each member of the food service staff will depend upon whether the courses are plated or silver service. For silver service, eight covers each is ideal, although ten is normal for experienced staff. When plate service is used the number is extended to 12.

Wine service staff can usually cope with about 20 to 25 customers each. If silver service is being used the wine service staff usually assist in the service of vegetables with the main course in order to speed up the service.

The top table is always served first and cleared first, the remaining tables then can take their cue from it. The signal to serve and clear is coordinated and given by the one person in charge of the function. The movement of staff during the service of the meal must be limited and orderly. This cuts down on the possibility of accidents, and creates a good impression. Only the wine service staff have the freedom to move around, keeping the wine glasses topped up.

When a meal has been served and the guests are having coffee, the food service staff will be withdrawn if there are to be speeches. Only the wine service staff remain to serve any drinks that may be required.

Party booking

When a special party booking is made it is important to record in detail the particular requirements of the guest in order that the function can be planned in advance to satisfactorily meet their requirements. A booking form or diary is used and the information recorded would include some of the following information:

Once the guests' requirements are recorded for a special party booking it is important to communicate clearly the details of the function to all appropriate staff. This special business notification is issued so that each department can plan in advance and not only see its own role but the role of other sections in the preparation for the special business.

```
┌─────────────────────────────────────────────────────────────┐
│ SPECIAL PARTY BOOKING                    DATE............    │
│                                                               │
│ TIME _____(ARRIVE) _____(MEAL) _____(DEPART)   │
│ ROOM _____        │
│ NUMBERS _____        │
│ TYPE OF FACILITIES REQUIRED _____        │
│           _____        │
│ NAME OF CLIENT _____        │
│ COMPANY _____        │
│ ADDRESS _____        │
│         _____        │
│ TELEPHONE _____        │
├───────────────────────────────────────────────────────────── │
│ MENU _____        │
│      _____        │
│ WINES _____        │
│ FLOWERS _____        │
│ TABLE PLAN                                                    │
│                                                               │
│ SEATING PLAN _____        │
│ DRINKS _____        │
│ CLOAKROOMS _____        │
│ LICENCE _____        │
│ M.C.(MASTER OF CEREMONIES) _____        │
│ PRICES _____        │
│ CONFIRMATION _____        │
│ REMARKS _____        │
│         _____        │
│         _____        │
└─────────────────────────────────────────────────────────────┘
```

The special business notification would include the following information:

Weddings

Weddings are an important part of function business and to ensure their success, attention must be paid to detail and procedure. The reception is

---

SPECIAL BUSINESS NOTIFICATION

CIRCULATE TO: LIST ALL THE PEOPLE CONCERNED
DIRECTLY AND INDIRECTLY
WITH THE FUNCTION

DATE _____
TIMES _____   THIS INFORMATION IS COMMON _____
    TO ALL CONCERNED _____
FUNCTION _____
NUMBERS _____
NAME _____

CHEF _____ DETAILS AFFECTING ORDERING AND FOOD PREPARATION

RESTAURANT
MANAGER _____ DETAILS OF THE MENU AND WINES TO BE SERVED
LAYOUT PLAN FOR TABLES
DRINK SERVICE
ETC

ACCOUNTS_____ DETAILS OF CHARGES

OTHER
DEPARTMENTS_____ SPECIAL REQUIREMENTS OTHER THAN THE ABOVE
INCLUDING CLOAKROOM FACILITIES, FLOWERS,
ENTERTAINMENT ETC

---

the medium by which the guests have the opportunity of meeting the bridal party. Once the wedding ceremony is over, whether it be in church or registry office, the bridal party leave first for the reception, to enable them to have their photographs taken before the other guests arrive. When all the guests have arrived, the bridal party should be arranged to receive them, either in a line or semi-circle depending on the size of the room, in the following order: the bride's mother and father (or representatives), the bridegroom's parents (or representatives), the bride, the bridegroom, the best maid, the best man. The guests should be announced by the person in charge of the function (maître d'hôtel or manager or mangeress).

The wedding cake can be placed in the reception room, and cut by the bride and bridegroom, after the guests have been introduced, or placed in the room where the final meal is taking place, and cut just before the coffee is served.

During the reception an informal toast is proposed to the bridal couple, after the guests have been served with a drink for this purpose. When the reception is over, the meal is announced. The guests should be directed to the dining-room, with the exception of the bridal couple. When all the other guests are seated, the bridal couple are led in by the person in charge,

Table layouts for special parties

who requests the guests to be upstanding, and the bride and bridegroom are applauded to their seats. The seating plan would depend upon the number of guests, but the arrangement of the top table is important, and, naturally, according to the wishes of the bride.

One popular arrangement for the top table is:

The Clergyman as Chairman, which is customary.

Seated on his right, the bride, the bridegroom, the best maid and best man
Seated on his left, the bride's mother, the bridegroom's father and the bridegroom's mother and the bride's father or their representatives.

In this case there is a total of nine persons, but if there are more the bride should decide where to place them.

During the service of the meal the bride must always be served first.

Speeches

1 Clergyman says grace.
3 Clergyman proposes the formal toast to the bride and bridegroom.
4 The bridegroom replies on behalf of his wife.
5 Toast to the bridesmaid.
6 Best man replies on her behalf.
7 Bride's father gives a vote of thanks to the chairman.

Drinks

One for the reception, one for the speeches and wine during the meal is the usual allocation.

After the meal and speeches all formality ends and there may be dancing or entertainment.

Self service

The concept of self service is by no means a new one and in the times of large private households with their own personal staff providing meal service, the traditional French style of service operated. In that style it was common for the elaborate dishes of food to be held out before the guest and they were expected to help themselves from the dish. The main reason for that style was to allow the guest to have control over their choice of type of food and quantity required.

There are various forms of self service in existence today. The extent to which the service is done by the customer himself will vary considerably. It is however rare to find a total self service operation where the customer is independent of service staff. It is more usual for the customer at some point to require assistance, even if this is limited to the clearing up afterwards or the collection of cash. Sometimes the self service element is very limited and only used as a form of encouraging customer participation to promote interest and enjoyment of the meal experience. Where a full waiter service system exists there is normally a great display of expertise that impresses the customer, and although participation does exist, particularly in guéridon service, the customer is generally passive.

Counter, cold buffet and carvery

The most common form of self service is found in cafeterias, and perhaps better known as counter service. In counter service the role of the waiting staff or floor staff is diminished and their main activity is the handling of equipment. The customer's dirty dishes and tables are cleared and a supply of clean trays, crockery, and cutlery are maintained. The activity of offering food and serving out food on to plates, is carried out by the counter staff who are usually the same staff who have prepared the food or beverages. The customer makes his own choice and carries his own food from the servery counter to a selected eating place.

The service skills required by staff are less complicated than in a full service but the organisation is no less important. The success of counter self service depends very much upon the design and layout of the servery counter. A smooth flow of service is essential and an understanding of the operations in a meal service activity is essential if the best layout is to be planned. Just as in any restaurant situation where the meal has a special sequence, so in self service must it follow an orderly routine.

The first activity is customer selection and a menu should be available, before the customer proceeds to select food he needs to have something on which to carry it, so a tray is the next most important item. As the customer moves along the service counter he should be able to select cold items first so that the time left for carrying hot dishes is kept to a minimum and any heat loss is reduced. After the meal has been chosen the cutlery can be collected that is required for eating the particular meal. Finally payment is made once the selection is complete. Other items such as condiments and napkins should also be left to the end. An after meal beverage such as coffee is commonly included in the service counter, but the better organisation will have a separate dispensing area for this and allow the customer to pre-pay. Thus the customer can be assured that after his meal he can enjoy a fresh hot beverage without having too much delay.

The layout of the counter is not the only factor that is important in ensuring a smooth service as bottlenecks can easily be caused by any lack of food or equipment on the counter. Similarly, service can be interrupted if tables are not cleared quickly. The floor service staff must work quickly to remove all used dishes immediately the customer has finished, and tables should be wiped clean. All the equipment must move as quickly as the customers, and in busy periods the supply of trays and cutlery must be maintained. A shortage of these items can cause chaos. One has to remember that some self service counter operations in institutions may not have a final cash payment and consequently may move much more quickly.

Whilst this form of self service is normally found in cafeterias that is not to say that it does not exist elsewhere. Self service is in fact a popular method of meeting the demands of fluctuating business when staff levels are low, and can be found in operation for breakfast in many hotels. Similarly when cold buffets are available it is usual for the customers to help themselves to food from the display. The extent to which this selection is self service will again vary. At breakfast for instance, it may only be the first course that is available from a counter and main dishes will often be waiter served.

When an elaborate cold buffet is on display the customers may have their meat served to them by a member of staff and only be allowed to select their own accompanying salads. Thus an element of portion control is retained.

The modern carvery was established to promote sales through greater customer participation, and originally the guest was allowed to attempt the complex skills of carving their own meat from a whole joint. Procedure will vary from one establishment to another as consequently will the related portion control and wastage factor. Some establishments will make extensive use of pre-portioned foods to control their issues, but this can tend to limit customer choice.

The principal advantages of self service are the saving in numbers of service staff and the reduction in complexity of skills required. These may not arise out of a difficulty in obtaining skilled labour or an inability to train but might merely be the consequence of a market where the customers average spend is so low that it is not profitable to have a lot of skilled waiting staff.

The principal disadvantage of self service is the lack of personal attention that the customer receives. There is also a disadvantage to the establishment arising out of the lack of portion control.

The real key to a good self service system is to be fully equipped, well planned and laid out with an attentive back up staff. The customers must not be allowed to feel that they are undertaking an onerous task in the absence of service staff. The guests must believe that they are having freedom of choice in pleasant surroundings that are clean, well equipped and well organised with the support of a friendly courteous staff. In good self service it is only the method that is different from full waiter service, all the other important factors are the same. Self service must be 'self selection' and certainly not 'do it yourself'.

Miscellaneous types of service

Lounge service

This type of service takes place in the lounges of residential hotels, and refers to the service of coffees, teas, sandwiches, afternoon teas, alcoholic and non-alcoholic beverages, which residents can generally have twenty four hours each day, if the staffing permits this service to be provided.

Non-residents can only have alcoholic beverages during permitted hours in accordance with local licensing regulations.

The lounge service staff operate generally from the still-room and dispense bar, which also serves the restaurant or dining-room. The duty hours can be long covering as it can, the twenty four hour period. Shifts are operated and it is usual for the duties to be covered at night time by the hotel portering staff, between eleven at night and seven in the morning. Night staff would serve lounges and private rooms if required.

The lounge service staff are responsible for the cleanliness of the lounge areas in which they operate, ensuring that the tables are kept clear and clean; if glass-topped, wiped down with a damp cloth. Chairs have to be kept brushed and carpets vacuumed.

Afternoon teas were a feature in many hotels, particularly the big holiday resort hotels. However many have now discontinued them for economic reasons but some establishments still serve afternoon teas on request. These meals used to be quite elaborate, a meal in themselves, giving a choice of sandwiches, hot muffins, hot sausage rolls, currant bread, preserves and a pot of tea. Three-tiered cake stands placed alongside the lounge tables were used to present the foodstuffs.

47

Today, lounge staff serve mainly teas, coffees, sandwiches and biscuits, and alcoholic and non-alcoholic beverages. These staff are normally under the supervision of the restaurant manager or headwaiter unless the establishment is large enough to support a head lounge waiter. The duties would be organised by the person responsible for the lounge staff.

Floor service (room service)

This type of service consists of serving meals, drinks, etc, to guests in their private rooms.

Floor service is still available in the larger hotels today, morning teas and breakfasts, however, tend to be the meals that are catered for. Breakfasts are mainly continental, consisting only of a hot beverage with rolls or bread. A number of establishments have tea- and coffee-making machines in guests' rooms or machines which are for vending alcoholic beverages. Fruit and biscuits are often left for guests and a personal room service not provided. This do-it-yourself catering in guests' rooms is popular with many guests and saves considerably on staff costs.

Floor service staff would normally operate from a pantry on the respective floor, which would be stocked with all that is necessary to serve a meal in a guest's room, or a suite of rooms.

A trolley, trays, cutlery, crockery, linen, glassware, cruets and other condiments, coffee, tea, sugar, etc, would be kept in a lockfast cupboard. A stock of wines, spirits and minerals may also be available. This pantry area would be equipped with refrigerator, sinks and a small cooker or hot cupboard. The main meal would be prepared in the hotel's central kitchen and sent up by lift (dummy waiter) to the pantry, floor service staff would also be under the supervision of the restaurant manager or headwaiter, unless the hotel was large enough to have a head floor waiter, who would organise and control his own floor service staff. Such a person would be responsible for the execution of all floor service orders.

Special situations

Food and beverage service can take place in a very wide variety of situations. The methods used in different situations will vary according to circumstances, although the same basic principles will always apply.

So far we have looked at restaurant and dining-room locations where the tasks of service are complex and the activity of service is fairly intense. If we were to attempt to define food and beverage service we would find that it is difficult to draw a clear line to indicate where the production operation ceases and the service activity begins. However, there are a number of situations where the conditions influence the method of service adopted, and it is worthwhile to look at the main influencing factors in these situations.

Industrial catering

The field of industrial catering should not be confined to providing a service solely for industrial complexes. Any situation where people are engaged in work as their main activity, whether it be in a factory or an office, indicates that the service they require is supplementary. This does not mean that it is unimportant in any way: the contrary is in fact true. If someone is to perform their job effectively, then the conditions under which they are fed are one of the influencing factors.

The common factors which emerge from a work situation are time and money. Most workers have a limited time in which to eat and the service should be fast. Although much of the feeding is subsidised, it requires to be run at fairly low cost and the result is that service staff require to be kept to a minimum. Hence in a large number of work situations, where mass feeding is involved, we tend to adopt a counter or self service method. There are of course exceptions determined by the priorities of the managers of work situations rather than by the caterer.

One of the most common exceptions to the fast mass feeding require-ment is the directors' dining-room situation. Many organisations require to provide hospitality to visiting executives, often in order to negotiate substantial business deals. It is common to discuss business over mealtimes, and a relaxed private atmosphere is sought. Thus we can find in industrial and commercial catering, situations which are very similar to first class restaurants, where a high degree of personal service is provided and the standard of food and beverage service demanded is complex. Great import-ance is placed on personal attention and a display of perfectly executed waiting skills.

In industrial catering it can be seen that the food and beverage service element is fundamental to effectiveness and morale at work, whether on the shop floor or at management level.

Institutional catering

It is never easy to classify catering situations without examples, and the term *institutional catering* itself does not give a clear picture of the situation. The term *welfare* is also sometimes used to classify a sector of the industry. A clearer picture of the special circumstances in which food and beverage service has to operate, is shown by examples of the specific type of institution concerned. Hospitals, schools, residential homes and penal institutions are some of the establishments in which the service is provided to complement a specific feeding requirement. The nutritional value of the food or beverage is carefully determined by the circumstances and the activity of feeding functional rather than incidental. Nevertheless the service activity is often a highlight of the day and has a bearing on morale. Social skills may come more to the forefront than technical ones.

Each of the above examples of institution has its own special service circumstances that are worth considering. Hospitals require to provide a food and beverage service not only for their patients but also for their employees. This service is often required for a twenty four hour period, and the numbers involved can be substantial.

The organisation of service for hospital patients is peculiar in as much as the movement of food is often to the immobile patient. A number of systems can be used, provided they satisfy the main requirements of this arrangement. Food and beverages that are required to be served hot have to be handled in such a way that the heat and quality are retained. Special equipment is required and the movement of food has to be highly organised. The skills of service, both technical and social are mastered by nursing staff whilst the supervision is normally done by a catering specialist.

Providing the service for hospital staff is not dissimilar from industrial catering and similar techniques are used. Like industry, the hospital service operates a diverse service, to meet the requirements of different levels of staff activity. Many large hospitals have facilities for special functions, conferences and social events, with the necessary food production and food and beverage service support. **Schools** provide an important food service, particularly to the young, where not only is a basic nutritional requirement met, but standards of conduct and behaviour are established. The food and beverage service activity is complementary to essential feeding process but nevertheless determines the efficiency with which the job is done. In secondary and higher education the requirements are different and the service technique changes to provide a more interesting type of service. Young people are always very discerning and the standards of service, whether personal or remote require to be high.

In other welfare establishments it is common for the customer to be disadvantaged, and require additional personal service. Providing a service to mentally or physically handicapped persons requires special skills both technical and social. Common to all forms of food service, however, is the need to recognise the customers' needs. A good member of service personnel is one who can adapt to a variety of changing circumstances, although it is usual for someone in a food and beverage service career to choose the sector of the industry in which they wish to remain and operate.

Transport catering services
When providing a service to people using transport by rail, road, sea or air, there are a number of common requirements to be met.

Firstly it is often necessary to operate within limited facilities. Sometimes there are constraints of time, with the customer being in a hurry to get from one place to another, it is not unusual for the customers to have a limited choice as to where and when they eat.

Road The form of transport by which the motorist has the greatest freedom of choice, and yet the service provided for motoring customers is one of the most often criticised, in particular the services provided for motorway users. Particular to the motorist, is the requirement for food and non-alcoholic beverage, rather than the provision of alcohol. Service has to be fast and there is little opportunity of predicting flow of business. Thus good service for road transport users, has to be spontaneous. A twenty four hour service is required and therefore shift systems of staffing are used.

Sea Perhaps the next form of transport in which the customer has some freedom of choice, particularly when cruising. To provide a service to customers who are using sea transport does not have the same difficulties as many other forms. The space is only limited to a certain extent, and the numbers although not precisely determined, fall into a predictable category. On short crossings or river cruising, the service is often limited, although beverage service can be extensive. On longer journeys, however, such as extended cruising, the service requires to be diverse. Large ocean going liners are often equipped like floating hotels and it is possible to provide a full first class restaurant service. Because of the nature of sailing, customers are regular and a high degree of personal service develops. The activities of restaurant, lounge and room service are much as described earlier.

Rail and air These both involve providing a service in difficult circumstances. The amount of space is limited, and so is the time. However, advance planning can operate as numbers are predictable and times of service pre-determined.

Airlines have in fact developed a highly sophisticated service and on long journeys in particular, the customer is guaranteed an adequate provision of food and beverage, with a friendly and courteous service. Airline staff are trained in the special social skills required, and have extensive practice of working in the confined conditions associated with aircraft. The standard of service provided can vary from a basic provision on short charter flights to a first class service on long distances in large or supersonic aircraft. The primary restriction is weight and therefore preparation of food is done at base mainly, with the activity on the aircraft being a service activity. Beverage service is a special feature, as travellers on intercontinental flights may take advantage of liquor duty exemption. With air travel being fairly expensive in Europe, food is often included in the travel cost.

The space restriction on trains is similar to aircraft, but there is not the same difficulty of weight. Thus it is possible to carry out food preparation on trains in specially designed compact kitchens. Because trains can carry very large numbers of passengers the service activity is not as easy. Unlike aircraft, the customers have a great deal of freedom of movement, and it is possible to have a static dining area or restaurant and buffet car. When compared with air travel, the cost of travel by rail is not great. However, the provision of food and beverage is an additional cost to the customer and therefore the standard is often measured against the cost. In Britain the cost of food and drink when travelling by rail can be fairly high, as the operating cost is high, it is common, therefore for people to make their own provision when using this mode of transport.

In train restaurant cars where full meal service is provided the service staff require to develop the same skills as in a large first class restaurant. Training is given to staff in special simulated restaurant cars, and practice is required in working in confined space in a moving vehicle.

In all forms of transport catering, there is an element of captivity with regard to the customer, and it is essential therefore for standards to be high or custom can be lost permanently.

Private clubs

These establishments cover a wide spectrum and the conditions of employment vary according to the type of club and the standards expected.

Clubs are normally controlled by a committee, composed of members, who define policy, and a steward or manager is expected to operate the club efficiently and profitably within that policy.

A percentage on food profits is often negotiated as an incentive. The expensive exclusive club with selected membership, may have bedroom accommodation for the use of members only, and other amenities such as squash, tennis, swimming or golf.

A high standard of food and beverage service would be expected. Club members can sometimes be more demanding and staff can be subjected to strong criticism from the members if service is not up to standard. This is where the three Ds are called for and discipline, discretion and diplomacy can help in dealing with such awkward situations.

Overall, the experience and financial rewards can be highly satisfactory in a club environment and there is a great deal of satisfaction to be derived from developing a career in an establishment where the clientèle are regular members and standards are high.

QUESTIONS

1 What are the basic rules of service?
2 What does 'cover' mean?
3 Describe three traditional forms of service.
4 What information is needed in advance of a banquet?
5 What is floor service?

ACTIVITIES

1 Sketch a long buffet table to show where you would position the different courses and plates and cutlery for a smooth flow of service.
2 Prepare a list of small equipment that a lounge waiter would require for the service of a full afternoon tea.

4
Preparation (Mise-en-place)

Preparation, or *mise-en-place*, the term commonly used in the hotel and catering industry, is essential whether it is the normal daily routine or a special function. It refers to the duties that have to be carried out by the members of the food and beverage staff. Rotas must be drawn up by the person in charge, who allocates the various duties, which should rotate, giving everyone the opportunity of doing different jobs.

Before the setting up of the room can begin, everything should be thoroughly cleaned every day, including the whole operational area. Carpets should be vacuumed, and chairs, tables, sideboards, glass doors, ledges, etc, wiped down with a cloth rinsed out with a mild bacteriacidal, and polished, before arranging the tables.

The clean crockery should be collected, and carefully checked for cracks, chips or any marks.

The cutlery, after it has gone through whatever process is used for cleaning, burnishing, polivit or silver dip, and been checked, can be put into service.

Clean linen must be collected from the linen room in exchange for soiled linen, and the tables once positioned can be covered with the clean cloths.

It is important to make sure that the table is clean and evenly balanced before clothing. The correct size of cloth must be used so that it fits squarely on the table, without dragging on the floor or creating a safety hazard.

To cloth the table correctly, stand between two of the legs with the folded cloth across the centre of the table, a correctly laundered cloth will have three folds, a single, a double and a single, in that order. These folds should be facing the person who is to cloth the table.

With the arms spread and holding the folds of the cloth between the thumb and first and second fingers, leave the bottom single fold free and allow it to drop over the far side of the table, with a gentle shake, draw the remainder of the cloth to the nearside edge and make certain that the table is neatly covered with the four points draping the legs of the table. Be careful not to crease the cloth by too much handling.

When setting up tables staff should always adhere to the strict rules of hygiene for the handling of crockery, cutlery and glass. Use a clean service cloth, for wrapping and carrying the cutlery, for carrying plates, and putting the final polish on them and on glasses.

Napkin folds

The Cornet (can be presented vertically or horizontally as a container for a roll, etc)

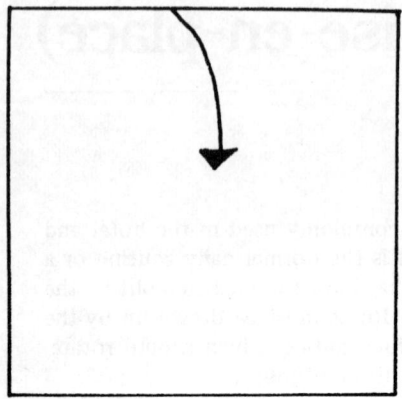

1 Top edge down two thirds

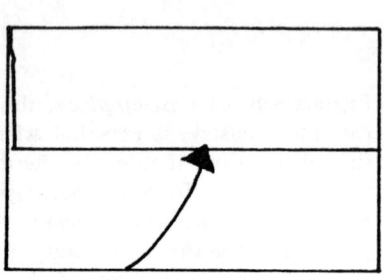

2 Bottom edge up to top edge

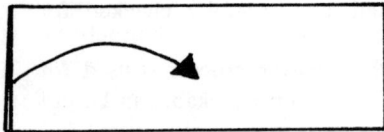

3 Left edge two thirds to right

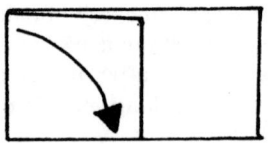

4 Top left corner to bottom centre

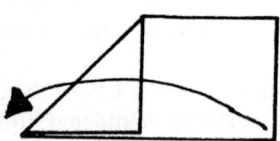

5 With left hand fingers inside fold wrap bottom right corner over to bottom corner

6 Fold both bottom corners up together

7 Open out base into circle to stand

8 Present on plate with flap facing guest

9 Can be laid horizontally to contain roll

When handling plates, use the rim only, avoiding the centre of the plate where food will be placed.

Lift cutlery by the handles only, and do not lift forks by the prongs, knives by the blades or spoons by the bowls.

When handling glasses only hold the stem and never the bowl out of which the guest will drink.

Staff will now proceed to lay the tables in accordance with the type of service being used.

The first item to be placed on the clothed table is the cover plate. The purpose of this plate is to provide correct positioning for the rest of the tableware, and it is important that it is correctly positioned otherwise the entire setting will lose its neat appearance. The cover plate should be placed approximately 2 cm (¾ in.) from the edge of the table in the centre of the space in front of the guest's chair. Next the different items of cutlery are placed on the table. To ensure that they are evenly spaced it is usual to place the innermost item first and work outwards at each side of the cover plate. Spacing between cutlery should be equal and each item should be straight. In good table setting technique it should not be necessary to later adjust the positioning of this cutlery.

Once all the cutlery is in position the side plate can be correctly positioned with its side knife. The glasses placed on the table at this stage are inverted so that they do not gather dust, and the napkins, once they are neatly folded are placed on the cover plate. Each place setting should be identical and have all the correct items that are required for either an a la carte setting or a full table d'hôte setting.

The tables are now completed with a cleaned and filled cruet and an ashtray if smoking is to be permitted.

There are two principal methods that can be used for table setting. In a busy restaurant which is organised along traditional lines, with each group of staff being assigned to a station, it is usual for these personnel to be responsible for setting the tables that they will be serving. An alternative method can however be used in which each member of staff has the responsibility for setting a particular item on all the tables in the room. This method will give a greater consistency of table setting and is a method that is commonly used when setting up large numbers of covers for special functions.

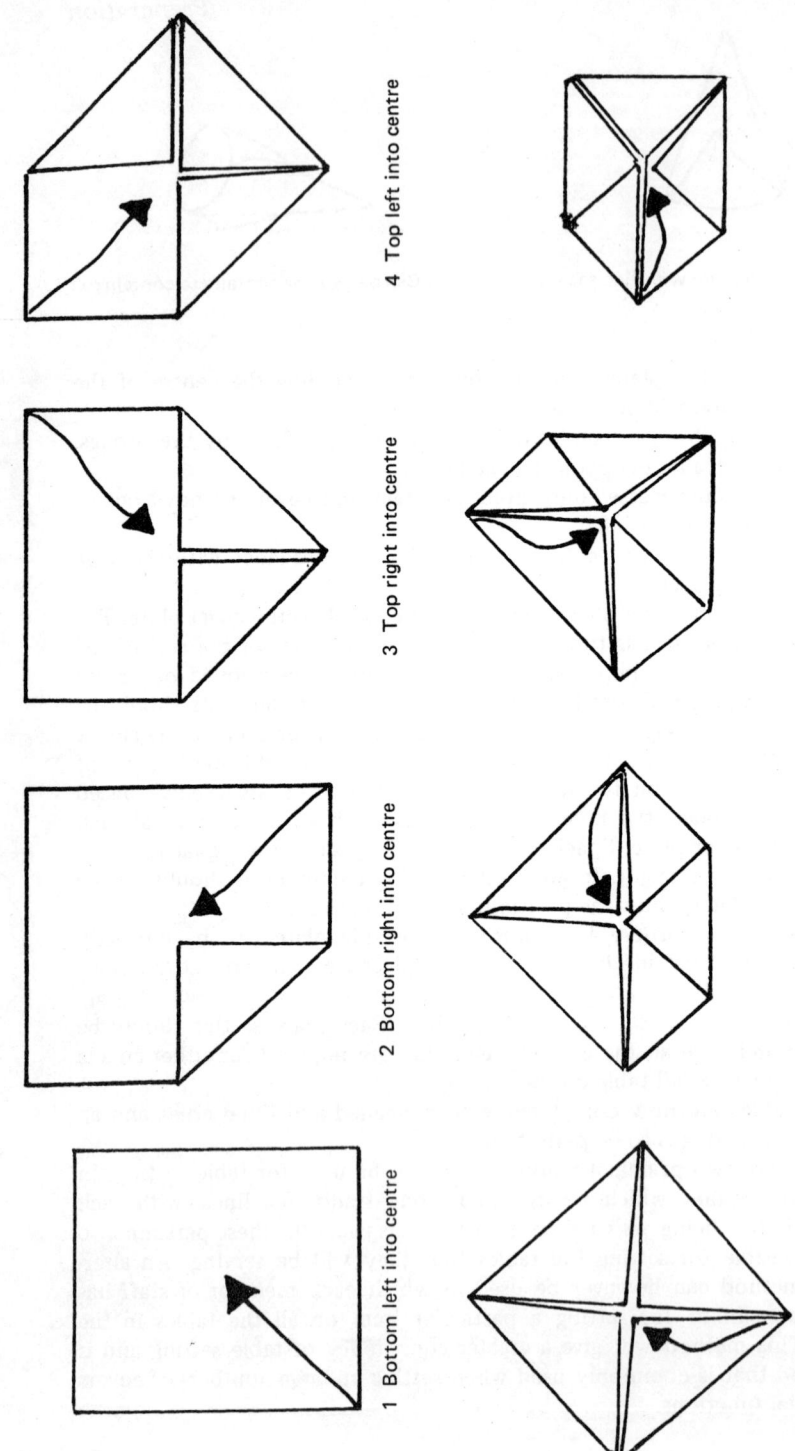

1 Bottom left into centre

2 Bottom right into centre

3 Top right into centre

4 Top left into centre

5 Bottom point into centre

6 Right point into centre

7 Top point into centre

8 Left point into centre

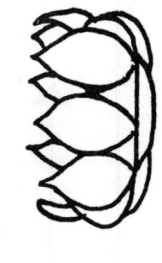

9 Turn whole napkin over

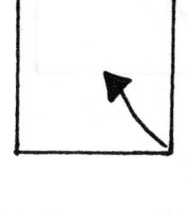
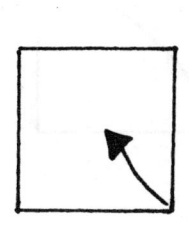

10 Bottom left into centre

11 Bottom right into centre

12 Top right into centre

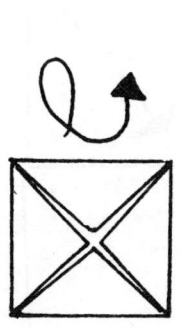

13 Top left into centre

14 Place on flat surface

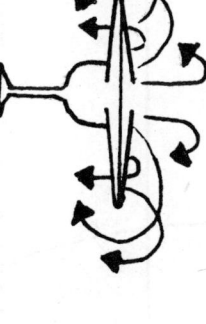

15 With glass on top, gently pull out and upwards, the eight loose points from the underside

16 Adjust the shape to resemble a rose or waterlily

The Rose or waterlily (used as a container for rolls, etc)

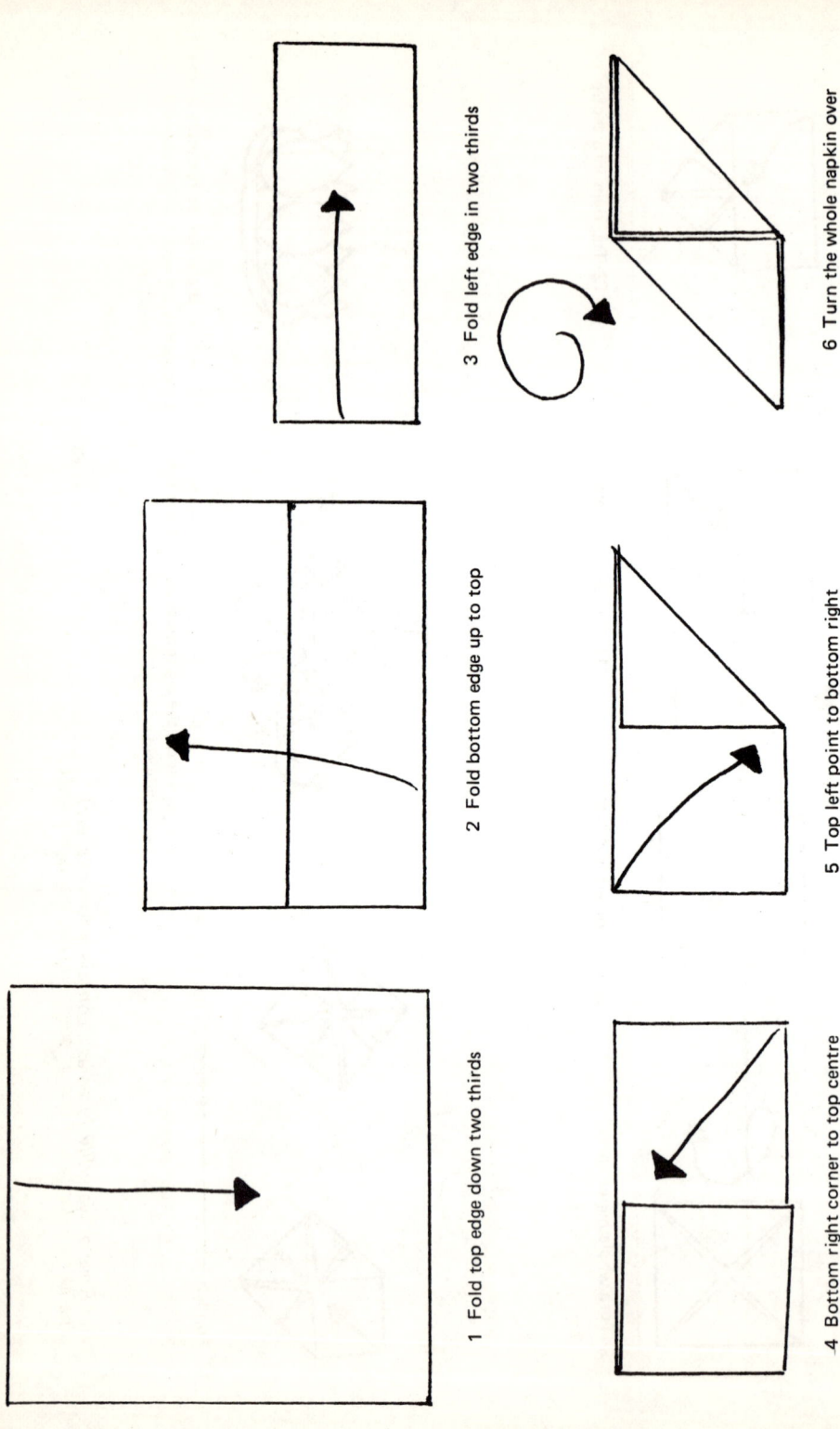

1 Fold top edge down two thirds

2 Fold bottom edge up to top

3 Fold left edge in two thirds

4 Bottom right corner to top centre

5 Top left point to bottom right

6 Turn the whole napkin over

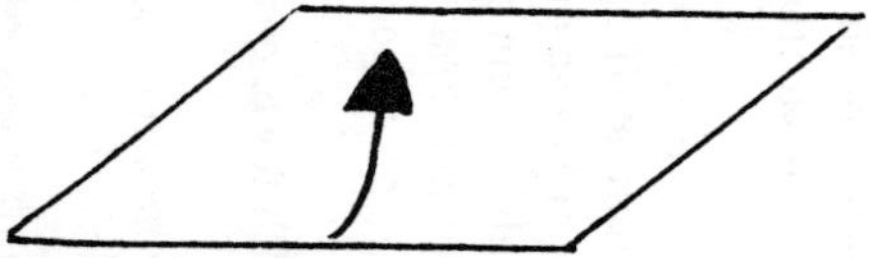

7 Bottom straight edge up to top edge

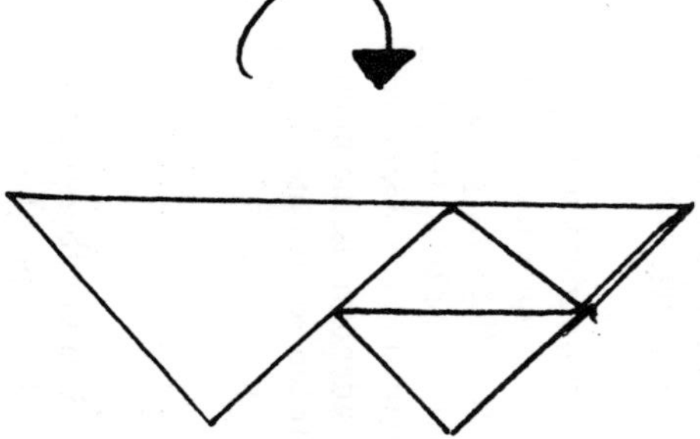

8 Rotate the peaks to the top

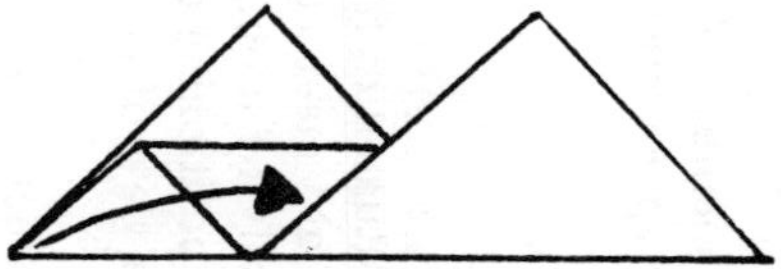

9 Tuck left point into centre fold

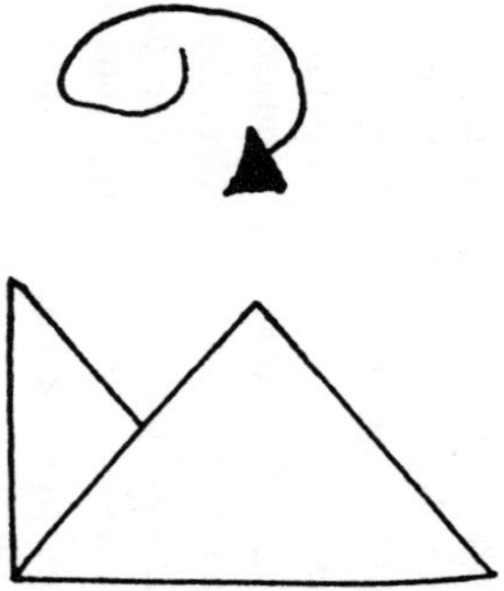

10 Turn the napkin over

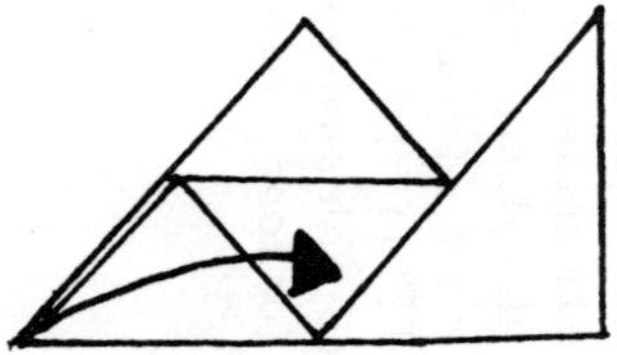

11 Tuck the left point into the centre fold

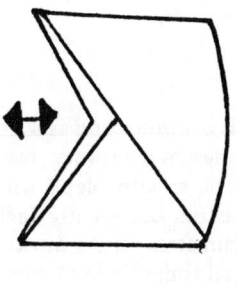

12 Open out the napkin from beneath to form a round base

The Mitre (placed in front of guest and can contain a roll)

Whichever method is used it is important that the member of staff in charge, inspects all tables to ensure that the overall appearance of the room is satisfactory.

Sideboards

A sideboard is a storage and service unit, conveniently situated to facilitate service. The design can vary but the basic style should meet common requirements, it should blend with the décor and ideally be mobile. One fitted with castors can greatly facilitate any change in positioning to meet changing circumstances. As most sideboards are in the view of customers they must at all times be kept neat and tidy.

Once the room has been set up satisfactorily, the sideboard has to be prepared for service. The sideboard should be stocked with the following items: extra plates, cutlery and linen for the re-laying of tables, an assortment of condiments relating to the menu of the day, including, mustards, sauces, pepper mill and appropriate accompaniments determined by particular dishes.

All the extra equipment should be placed in the appropriate sections. There ought to be drawers for cutlery, lined with baize to reduce noise, and shelves for plates. Linen can be kept in a cupboard. If a hot plate is incorporated in the sideboard this should be switched on prior to service.

Where a full silver service is to operate it is important that the sideboard is fully stocked with service spoons and forks. The sideboard is the main service point for food service staff, between the kitchen service area and the customer.

Stations

A station is a section of the room which is allocated to members of the restaurant or dining-room staff, and depending on the type of service being provided, whether plated, silver or gueridon service could encompass between four and six tables. The average number of guests to be served would be in the region of twenty.

The restaurant manager, headwaiter or supervisor will first of all inspect and check that all the preparatory duties have been carried out satisfactorily, then staff will be assigned to their respective stations.

In most establishments there are some stations that are more desirable than others and therefore it is common practice to rotate staff and give everyone experience of all aspects of the room. However, it is also practical to give senior staff permanent stations because of their ability and skills to cope with more customers, and the fact that there may be regular customers who have a preference for a particular table and expect to be served by the same member of staff.

Junior staff are often given their initial experience with fewer customers in less public or busy parts of the room.

Ideally each station should have its own sideboard from which to work, but in some circumstances two stations may have to share. This can cause difficulties during busy periods and every effort must be made to work together as a team, making certain that the top of the sideboard is kept clear and that dirty crockery and serving dishes are removed as quickly as possible. The golden rule is, *'never leave the room empty-handed, always look around to see if anything unnecessary can be dispensed with — use your head and save your legs.'*

Once stations have been allocated it is the responsibility of the staff to ensure that everything is ready for service to begin.

Closing duties

At the end of service closing duties have to be carried out in the restaurant.

The tables must be cleared and stripped of their cloths, ashtrays emptied into a fireproof container, chairs should be upended and stacked on top of tables.

All electrical equipment must be switched off and disconnected. Sideboards should be cleared of all their equipment, cutlery, crockery and linen. These items should be put away in lockfast cupboards. Cruets and sauces should be put away in their respective storage places.

If the dining-room is to be used for breakfast on the following day, some essential preparation must be done the night before. The required number of tables would be laid with clean cloths and, for a full English breakfast, the cover would be similar to a table d'hôte setting, but without the soup spoon. The fish knife and fork, joint knife and fork, sweet spoon and fork, and side plate and knife would be placed on the table. In place of glasses, teacups and saucers would be laid out with the cup inverted so as not to gather dust. Sufficient additional cutlery, linen and accompaniments would be left in the sideboards. A slip cloth should be laid over the table overnight.

A good mise-en-place is important at this time as breakfast service often requires to be fast, and it can be one of the most complex services due to the large number of items that have to be taken to and from the guest's table in the course of the meal.

Accompaniments

Accompaniments are various sauces, seasoning, etc, served with food to improve its flavour. No dish is complete unless it has its correct accompaniment. The service of accompaniments is the responsibility of the restaurant staff.

The main purpose of an accompaniment is to enhance the flavour of a dish, but it is an optional extra and should be offered to the guest who is free to accept or decline it. An accompaniment is differenct from a garnish which is an integral part of a dish and incorporated in the presentation of that dish by the kitchen staff. Accompaniments fall into a number of categories, including, hot sauces, cold sauces, condiments and adjuncts. Some of the more regularly used accompiments include the following:

Dish	Accompaniment	Service
Hors d'œuvres	Oil and vinegar	Left on table
Caviar	Blinis or hot toast Half lemon wrapped in muslin Finely chopped onion Finely chopped parsley	Offered and served
Paté de foie gras	Hot toast and butter	Placed on table
Half grapefruit and grapefruit cocktails	Caster sugar	Sugar sifter left on table
Iced melon	Caster sugar and ginger	Offered separately Spooned on to plate Ratios of 4:1 sugar: ginger
Oysters, whitebaits, Smoked salmon and Other smoked fish	Buttered brown bread, Lemon wedges or quarters	Plate left on table Lemon served from dish
Snails	Buttered brown bread or Fingers of white bread	Plate left on table
Green pea soup	Croutons	Offered and served to Customer
Minestroni	Grated parmesan cheese	Sprinkled over soup
Bortsch	Sour cream, beetroot juice Small Bouchées of duck paste	Offered separately
Prawn cocktail	Buttered brown bread	Plate left on table
Poached salmon	Hollandaise sauce	Served to customer
Cold salmon or cold Lobster	Mayonnaise sauce	Served to customer
All deep fried fish	Tartare sauce and lemon Wedges	Served from sauce boat Lemon served from dish
All grills	Various sauces, bottled sauces And various mustards	Served from sauce boats Bottled sauces left on Table
Irish stew	Worcester sauce, pickled red Cabbage	Red cabbage served Sauce left on table
Jugged hare	Red current jelly	Served to customers
Curries	Poppadums, bombay duck Mango chutney, and other Adjucts including banana, Apple, coconut, etc.	Offer and serve separately To customer
Roast beef	Mustard, horseradish sauce	Served to customer
Roast lamb Roast mutton	Mint Sauce or Redcurrant jelly	Served to customer
Boiled mutton	Caper sauce	Served to customer
Roast pork Roast duck Roast goose	Sage and onion stuffing Apple sauce	Served to customer
Roast poultry	Bread sauce, game chips	Served to customer

Dish	*Accompaniment*	*Service*
Roast turkey	Cranberry sauce	Served to customer
Roast game	Bread sauce, game chips, Fried breadcrumbs	Served to customer
Spaghetti Macaroni Ravioli Gnocchi	Grated parmesan cheese	Sprinkled over pastas
Savouries	Cruet consisting of salt Pepper, mustards, worcester Sauce, pepper mill	Placed on table
Hot and cold sweets	Caster sugar, cream	Placed on table

Note
Other unusual or specialist dishes will have their own accompaniments determined by customer acceptability.

Menu knowledge

Before food and beverage staff can begin the service, it is important that they have a good knowledge of the menu, that they are going to serve.

An important part of the preparation before service includes a discussion of the menu. It is normal practice for the headwaiter or person in charge to have this discussion to ensure that all staff are familiar with the dishes of the day.

As the purpose of a menu is to communicate it is important to realise that this communication is between not only the waiter and the customer, but also between dining-room and kitchen. Menus are often written with special names or terms on them so that the kitchen can quickly recognise which dish is required and with which sauce or garnish. The information on the menu has often to be presented to the guest by the waiter who must fully understand it.

The menu, sometimes referred to as the 'bill of fare' or 'carte du jour', contains several important facts for the guest, namely: the type of food available, the method of cookery, the style of garnish, and the particular piece or cut of meat or fish. All of this information can readily be obtained by reading the menu. There is however other information that the guests might require in relation to their meal and this often has to be provided by the waiter. This additional information might include: the appearance of the dish, the portion size, the origin of the dish, the time for cooking, the degree of cooking required, and the predominating flavour. This last factor is of great importance to the guest.

The waiter therefore has a special job. This job is referred to as dish description. The function of dish description is to convey accurate information in consumer terms to promote the immediate sale and continuing sale through the general promotion of gastronomy. To perform the job of dish description properly the waiter needs to carry out four tasks:

Preparation

1 He must study the menu to see what is available.
2 He should research to find the content of each dish. This information will originate from the kitchen via the head waiter. It is important that the service staff know exactly what is going to be in each dish on that particular day, and they should not make any assumptions.
3 He should translate this information into the easily understood language of the customer. It is a common fault to use technical terms to describe dishes, forgetting that the customer does not always understand such terms.
4 Now the waiter is ready to describe the dish to the customer. This should be done in such a way that the customer is fully informed and better able to make his choice.

As part of the preparation before service, the headwaiter should ask some of his staff to describe menu dishes as they would do to the customer. This activity is sometimes called the menu lecture if trainees are involved, and includes checking that the correct accompaniments are known.

With more experienced staff, it is sufficient to check that they are familiar with any particular dish of the day (plat du jour).

QUESTIONS

1 List the mise-en place duties prior to service.
2 Name the cutlery used in a table d'hôte setting in the order in which it should be laid on the table.
3 What is a sideboard used for?
4 What is the golden rule when clearing a station?
5 What is an accompaniment?

ACTIVITIES

1 With some colleagues, set up four tables with four covers on each using the two different methods, each doing your own, then as a team where each person does a particular item. Compare the time required and the standards of table setting.
2 Select a menu and write out a list of the accompaniments that should be served with each dish. Then describe the main dishes as you would do to a customer.

5
Food Service

Serving the meal

The service of a meal takes a certain amount of skill, depending on the type of service. Time should always be spent on training staff to improve standards.

Serving at table requires good balance and fast reflexes. Good balance is required for carrying plates and serving food and beverages in the restaurant, and for movement in and out of the service area. Fast reflexes are required to avoid collisions and accidents. Silver service demands more technical skill as each item of food is served with a spoon and fork, the manipulation of which can be learned and mastered with practice.

When approaching to serve food at the table, from the left, the waiter/waitress should be perfectly balanced and alert, in the event of a customer turning round quickly without warning, resulting in serious consequences.

The correct position to adopt is to stand sideways, with the left foot forward. Bend from the hips and hold the serving dish flat on the left hand on a service cloth, which should be folded to prevent the hot dish causing burns. This service cloth should only cover the hand and arm and not hang loose or come into contact with any items on the table.

The dish should be held level and as near to the plate as possible to prevent gravy or sauce from spilling. Should food slip from the grip of the spoon and fork it will merely fall back on to the serving dish. Careful manipulation of spoon and fork and good positioning will prevent any spillage on the table, customer or floor. The presentation of food on the customer's plate is extremely important. It should be made to look appetising and attractive. Mastery of the manipulation of spoon and fork for service is the key to successful silver service.

If the food breaks up when being served the waiter or waitress should take the time and care to put the broken pieces together carefully, restoring them to their original presentation. When serving the main course of a meal, the meat or fish items should be placed on one half of the plate with the vegetables and potatoes that are to accompany the food being placed on the other part of the plate. It is important to avoid piling vegetables on top of the main meat or fish.

Soup which is already plated should always be placed on the table with the use of an underlay plate which serves a number of useful functions. Primarily the underplate makes it convenient to carry the hot plate of soup without the waiter's fingers touching the rim of the soup bowl or plate. It also improves the presentation of the dish, particularly when a small bowl is used for soup.

Clearing of plates

Plates should not be cleared from the table until all the guests have finished their meal, as this would cause embarrassment to a slow eater and disrupt the social function of a group of people eating together. To do so would make people feel that they were holding back the service, with the consequence that they might leave some of their food and not enjoy the meal to the full.

Good service should be relaxed and smooth.

After the guests have finished the waiter should remove the used plates by lifting them from the table with his right hand and placing them into his left hand where they can be stacked and carried safely. The stacking of plates is important and where a number of plates are involved this is done systematically to reduce the number of journeys required to and from the table. Clearing left-over food from one plate to another and sorting used cutlery can be done during clearing if the waiter turns away from the table to do so.

After the main course has been eaten and the dishes have been cleared, the table is prepared for the next course which is usually dessert. Cruets and butter are removed and the guests' side plates and knives taken away if they have finished with them.

The table is crumbed down with a clean napkin and a plate to catch the crumbs. This must be done as unobtrusively as possible and the guest must not be made to feel that he has made undue mess on the table. The waiter will discreetly remove the crumbs so that he can lay the necessary cutlery for the following course. If the customer has chosen cheese, then a new side plate and knife are laid with a fresh dish of butter. For dessert the spoon and fork are positioned at right and left of the guest ready for use.

After dessert, the table is completely cleared and crumbed down if necessary for the service of coffee.

Coffee cups and saucers with small underplates would then be placed in front of the guests from the right. Sugar should be offered and served from the left, then the dish placed on the table. The guests should be offered coffee to their own particular taste, with or without milk or cream.

Service of coffee

The guest should be approached from the right and the tray with the coffee pots held down close to the cup. The coffee should be poured first and milk added if required. The technique of pouring requires the waiter to tilt the pot by the handle and pivot it on the tray. In this way he has control of the pot with the right hand and the left hand bears the weight of the pots. If cream is to be served with the coffee it is normally left on the table for the guest to serve himself as required. Fresh coffee should be offered and may be left on the table if the guest requires it.

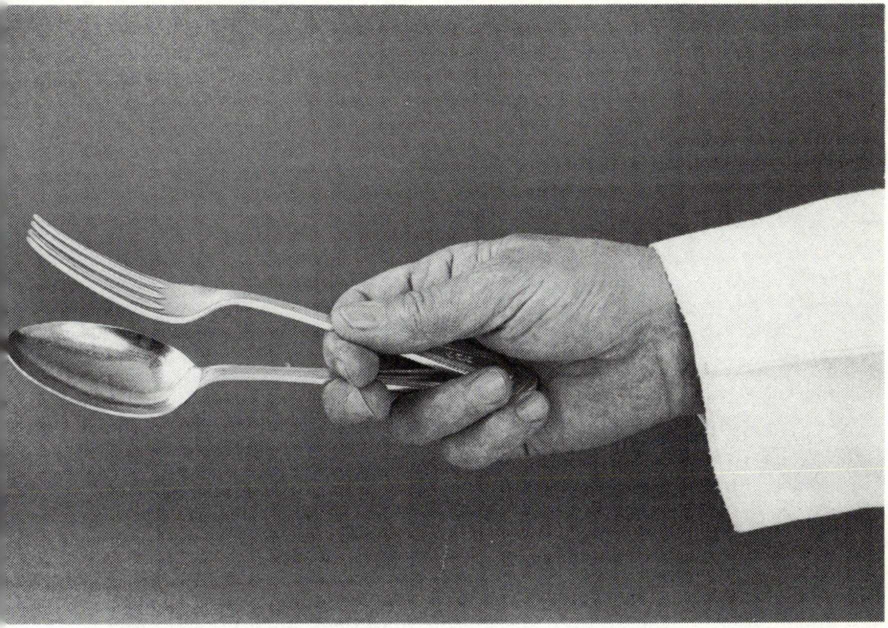

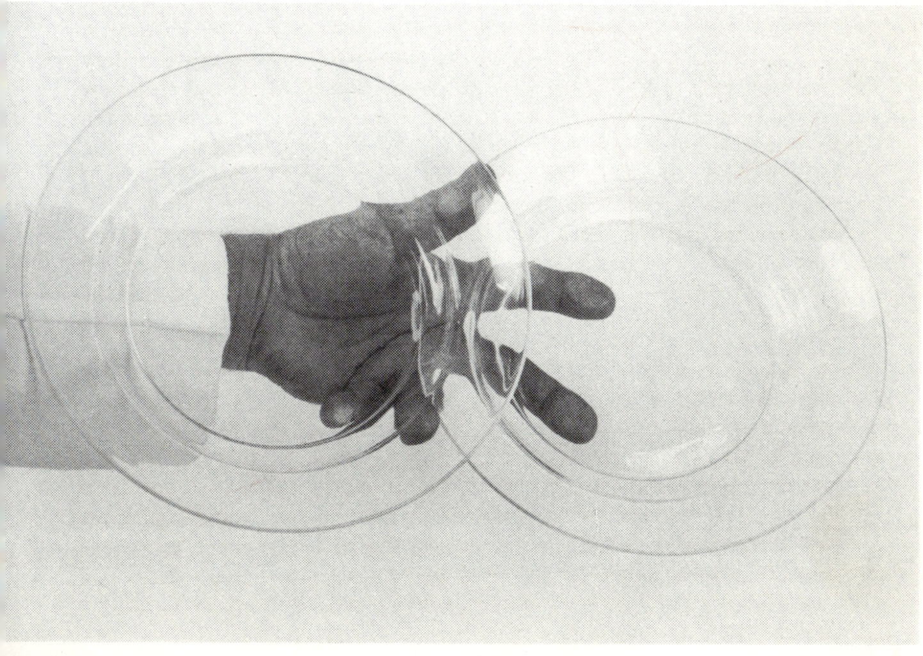

Serving the complete meal

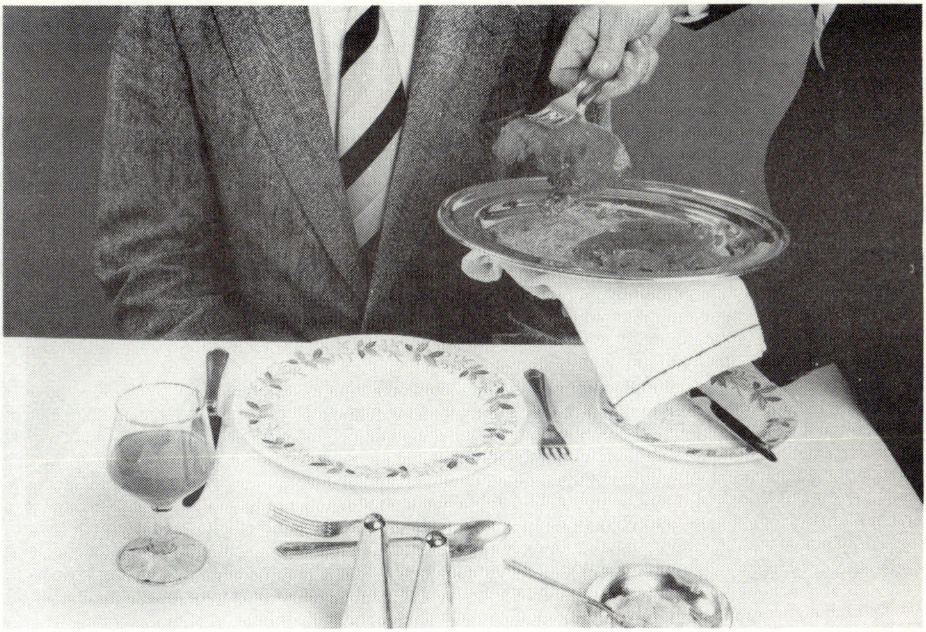

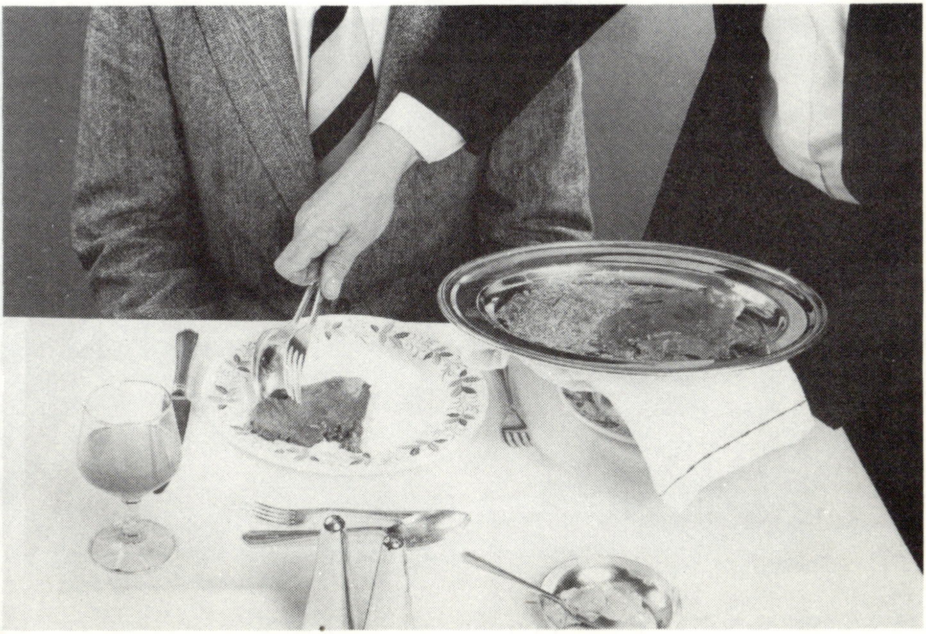

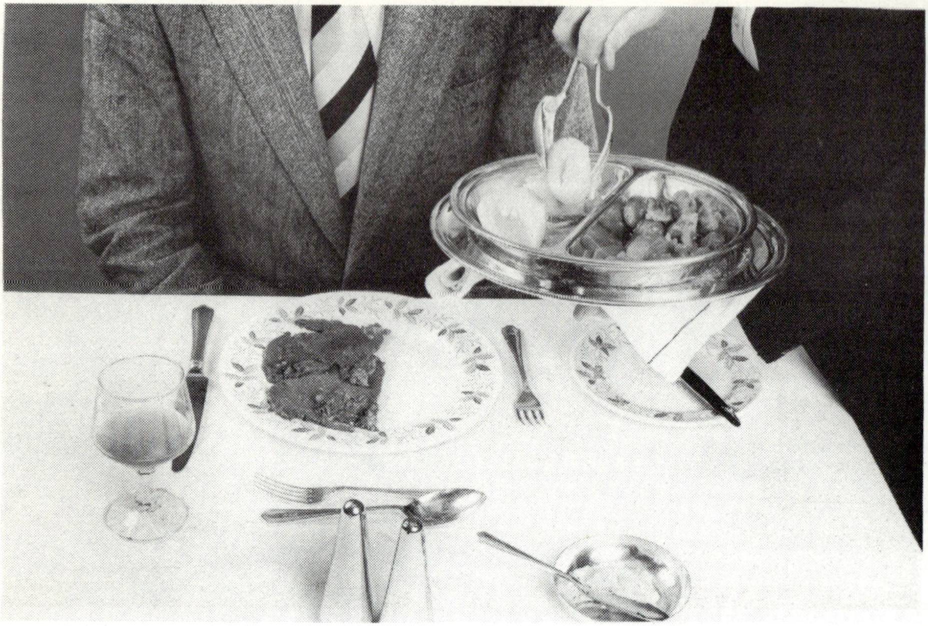

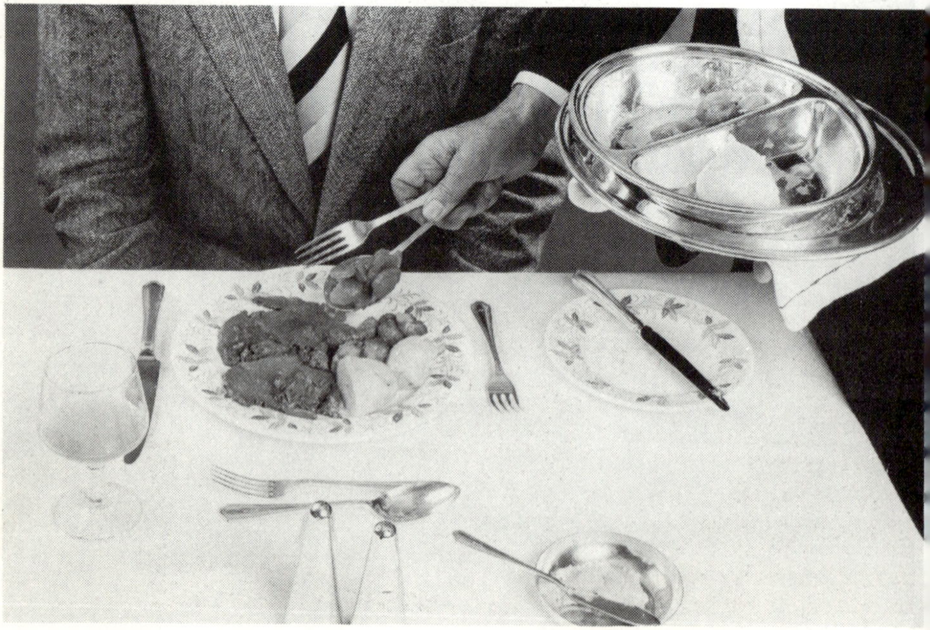

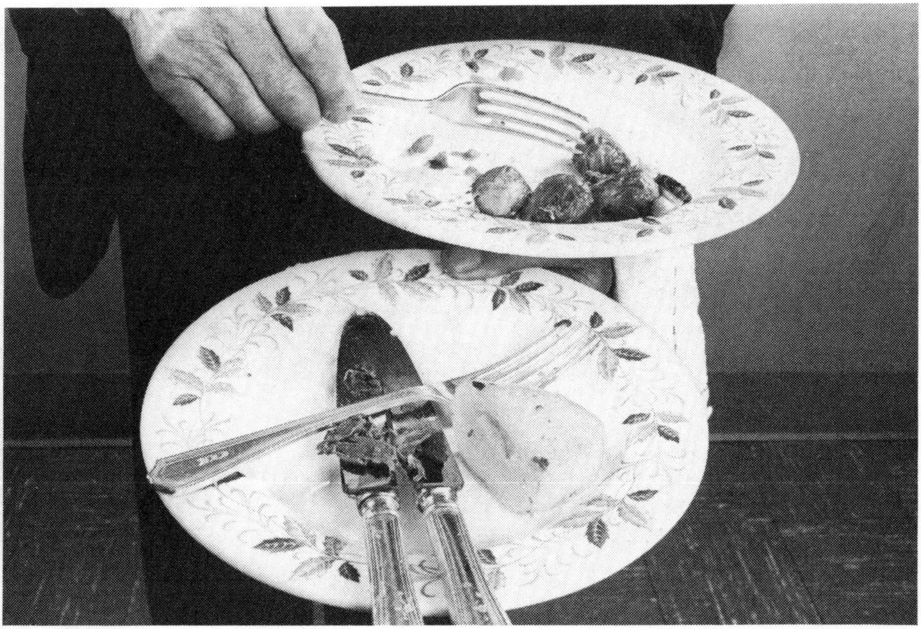

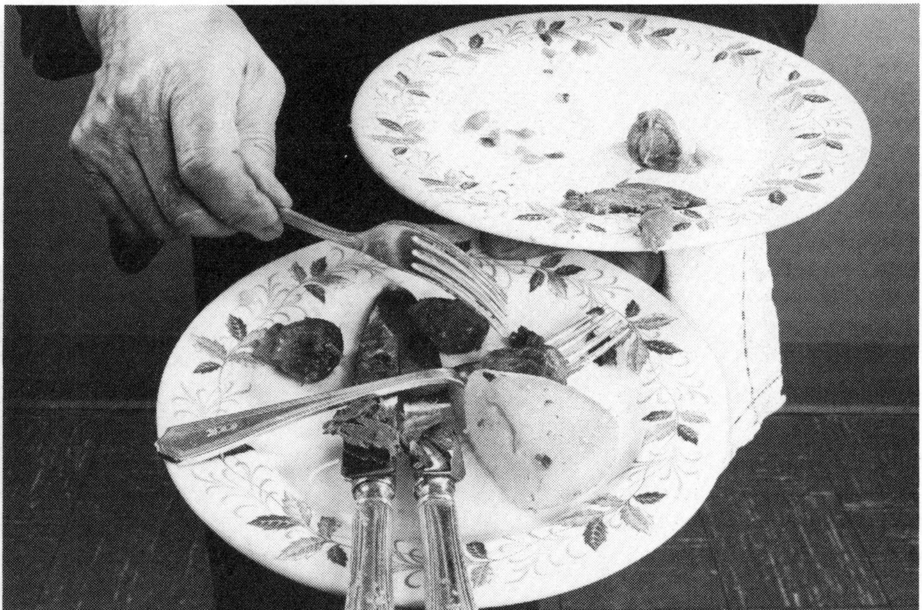

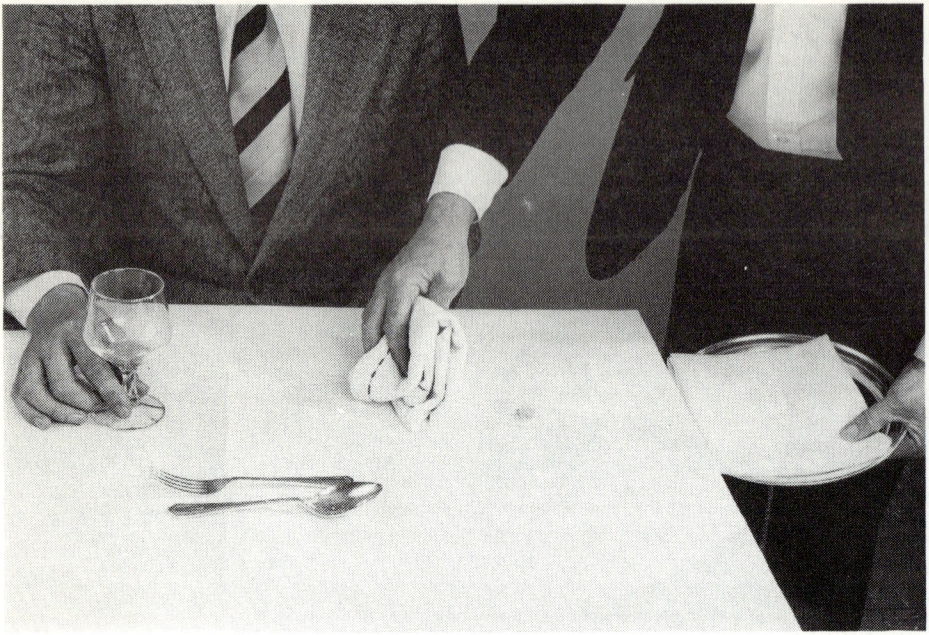

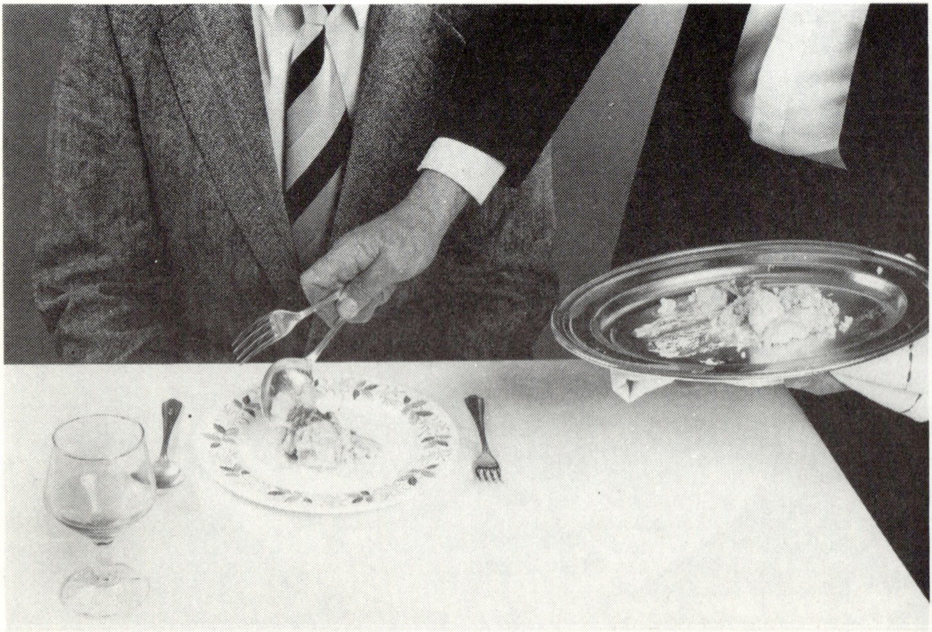

The aim of the food and beverage staff is to provide an efficient and unobtrusive service to the customer. The type of operation would decide on the style of tables and booths. Round tables are generally chosen for the luxurious intimate type of restaurant. Square and rectangular tables are more often found in popular catering establishments.

Booths were originally found in snack bars, cafes and cafeterias. However, they have now become accepted in all types of restaurant. The main advantage of a booth arrangement is that it gives a certain amount of privacy to the customers. The disadvantage is that the seating is fixed and the layout permanent with service difficulties with regard to access to the customer. In such an arrangement silver service becomes difficult to operate and a plated service is often used. This type of seating is popular with customers and now widely used. Tables which can be converted in size to accommodate different sizes of party are particularly useful.

Whatever designs are used for table arrangements, the primary consideration is customer convenience and comfort.

There must always be reasonable access for service and safe working arrangements. Adequate space is required between tables to prevent accidents.

The movement of service staff in the dining area has a bearing on the efficiency of the table service provided. Time and motion studies would have a great deal of relevance in connection with the layout and planning of the service stations. The activity of the serving staff must be organised to make the best use of time. If the waiter cultivates a good retentive memory then the taking of orders can be greatly speeded up, as each customer's individual choice can be remembered.

The serving of the correct dishes and their accompaniments in the correct sequence will improve the service. Anticipation and good timing of the various courses will save unnecessary journeys to and from the kitchen.

Unusual circumstances

Invariably during the service period there are a number of incidents that can take place unexpectedly and the service staff must be prepared to meet the requirements of these unusual circumstances. These are situations in which discretion, discipline and diplomacy are invaluable.

If a guest becomes ill the staff must remain calm and make the customer feel as comfortable as possible. While waiting for medical attention to be provided, the guest should not be given any stimulant, unless his illness has been professionally diagnosed. It is desirable to have at least one member of staff fully qualified and certificated in first aid and a first aid kit readily available. It is important to keep the service and atmosphere as normal as possible for other customers in the restaurant. In the case of a guest choking, it is essential for all food service staff to be trained in the correct action to be taken, as immediate action can be vital in this particular type of situation.

Handicapped customers must be shown every consideration, and special seating arrangements made. Where possible they should be allocated to tables near to the entrance, to reduce the difficulty of access or emergency exit. During the service of the meal they should be discreetly assisted where required, and when they indicate that they are willing to receive such assistance. With blind persons the waiter can quietly announce when each dish has been fully served before the appropriate guest.

Elderly guests may also require special attention or assistance. Hospitality and good service embrace all ages and types of guests whether young or old, familiar or unfamiliar, and a smile works wonders in a difficult situation.

If the restaurant caters for very young children it should be equipped to provide high chairs or special crockery and cutlery.

The disciplining of children is the responsibility of the people accompaning them, but experience has shown that staff should be ready to assist in maintaining order. Children should not be allowed to run around the restaurant in case of accidents. They should be kept from causing annoyance to other guests.

If a customer is intoxicated or becomes so in the restaurant, a great deal of diplomacy is required. Should he be causing a disturbance he may be asked to leave and, after settling the bill, be escorted from the premises. An intoxicated person should not be admitted initially, but there may be difficulties with people who are already in the establishment. The laws with regard to licensing must be strictly observed and the guide lines as to the admission of such persons clear to all the staff.

Hygiene and sanitation

The rules of sanitation cannot be stressed too highly or too often. The consequences of inefficient hygiene practices can have very serious medical repercussions. The effect on business can be far reaching, expensive and create a bad image. Such a bad image will take a long time to eradicate. It is therefore essential that everyone concerned with food and beverage service has a high awareness of the hazards of poor hygiene.

Each individual has a share in the responsibility to the public to prevent the contamination of foodstuffs and the spread of bacteria. They exercise this responsibility through adopting clean habits and always observing safe and hygienic practice. Food service staff in particular must have hands thoroughly washed and nails scrubbed at all times, and in particular after using toilet facilities. The use of a bacteriacidal gel in hand washing is advisable. Any cuts or burns must be treated and covered with the appropriate hygienic dressing.

If staff have coughs or colds these should be treated to prevent the spread of infection. Any person who has an infectious disease should be kept away from food areas.

Where food is put on display in the restaurant it should be treated in the same hygienic way as it would be in a shop, and appropriately covered or refrigerated as necessary.

Buffet displays must not have raw foods in proximity to fresh or cooked foods that are ready for consumption. Material used on buffet displays that is not consumable should not come into close contact with foodstuffs. When handling any foods serving cutlery or tongs must be used wherever possible. All equipment and display stands, tables or trolleys must be kept scrupulously clean at all times.

Management and staff must play their part in keeping a watchful eye on any hidden areas that can be a source of contamination. The restaurant and its service areas must be of a sufficiently high standard of cleanliness that they are not an attraction for pests, vermin or bacteria.

Animals should never be allowed in food preparation or service areas.

Food service staff should have separate protective clothing when they are not actually serving customers. During mise-en-place and other preparatory tasks an apron or protective coat should be worn. Staff can then change into their service uniform just before service.

There is a duty to maintain the highest standards of hygiene and staff should be trained to 'think clean for hygiene'. The penalties for poor hygiene can be severe and include closing down of the establishment.

Safety

Hygiene and safety are closely linked, particularly in a service operation. Many hidden dangers exist in a service area with regard to safety of the customer and staff member.

There should be adequate spacing between tables and chairs and passageways for the movement of staff and customers.

Staff should walk smartly and never run in the restaurant.

Other people's movements should be anticipated, and a look out kept for obstacles lying on the floor beside chairs, such as guests' briefcases or handbags. These should be placed where they will not cause a hazard and the guest should be tactfully asked to move them if necessary.

Never attempt to carry too much. Stack dishes carefully on trays and avoid overloading, keeping the weight evenly distributed.

Clean items should be kept apart from dirty items and glasses kept away from other dishes.

When removing dirty dishes from the table keep within your limitations and do not attempt to clear too much at one time.

In the event of an accident, while clearing the table or serving, immediate action should be taken. If there is spillage on the table the stain can either be covered with a clean napkin or slip cloth or the table cloth may need to be changed completely and replaced with a clean cloth.

If the spillage is on the floor it is equally important to have it cleared up immediately so that no one will slip on it. Food that has fallen on the floor must be lifted and disposed of at once in such a manner that it is obvious to the guest that it is going to be destroyed and not re-cycled.

When handling equipment, such as crockery, glass or cutlery, particularly in the presence of guests, this must be done hygienically and safely.

Any items from which the guest is to eat, must be handled as little as possible. Thus handle plates only by the rim, glasses by the stem or base, and cups or cutlery by the handles.

Complaints and compliments

Frequently a guest will wish to make comment to service staff. These comments may be of a complimentary nature or otherwise. Whatever is the situation, it is important that staff are trained to be good listeners and to deal correctly with complaints. A good communication between the service staff and the customer is the key to dealing with such a situation.

If there is a hold-up in the kitchen, the customer should be reassured that he has not been forgotten. Never argue with the customer, whatever the provocation, as this creates a bad image. It can embarrass other guests and be bad for business. In any difficult situation the customer should be made to feel that the situation is under control and that his interests are being considered. This general principle should be applied to situations of complaint, accident, illness and most other incidents.

Presentation of the bill

The bill for the guest's meal should normally be presented on request. There are some situations where it is kept available on the table for the guest and only requires updating. This is common practice in quick service operations where the customer is frequently in a hurry. In a first class restaurant, the pace is generally more leisurely and therefore on the host's request his bill is prepared from the information on the checking system, and it is presented to him at his table. The waiter who presents the bill is familiar with the meal that has been served and he has a responsibility to check that the bill is a fair representation of the service. If an item has been missed he should have the bill corrected. Similarly if the guest was dissatisfied with an item and returned it, the bill should make the correct charge. Many establishments will extend the responsibility of the service staff to make good any shortages on bills which arise through error or guest default.

Once the bill has been checked it should be folded to conceal the total with a corner folded back for easy opening. The bill is placed on a small tray or plate and given to the host by placing it on the table beside him. He then may pay either the waiter or the cashier according to the policy of the establishment.

The guest will pay his bill by cash, cheque, credit card or he may merely sign it so that an account can be forwarded. Service staff should be familiar with the establishment's policy with regard to payment. They must know what types of credit card are acceptable and how to handle them.

Gratuities

The payment of gratuities to service staff tends to cause a general dissatisfaction amongst staff. Traditionally it provided the guest with an opportunity to reward staff for outstandingly good service, and the system was adopted in restaurants whereby these gratuities were pooled and shared out amongst the service staff on a basis of seniority or length of service. However, the gratuities tended to be used to support poor wages and did not generally pass on any benefit to staff who were behind the scenes. This pooling or 'Tronc system' is still in operation in some establishments today.

Many customers now feel, however, that they are paying enough with increasing costs, service charges and taxes. To give additional gratuities or 'tips' is less common. However, good service is always appreciated and rewarded accordingly.

Food and beverage staff still do often depend upon gratuities to supplement their wages and most establishments operating a service charge system will ensure that the appropriate service staff receive their share. Customers sometimes resent the addition of a ten or fifteen per cent service charge if the service is indifferent.

The fact that these gratuities whether given directly by the guests as 'tips' or through the service charge system, are taxable, makes it important to have a fair system for the collection and pooling of them.

The paperwork of waiting

Control

Control is a word commonly used in any business enterprise to describe a system or a number of systems set up to let the management and key staff know what is happening to goods and services and the related income. The form which this control system takes will vary considerably with the type of operation. In a food and beverage service context we have two main areas in which our control takes place. The first or primary control is concerned with tracing what happens to the materials used in the operation. Thus we need paperwork to help us show the movement of food and beverages in our operation.

The secondary control is used to ensure that the correct revenue related to these foods and beverages is obtained from the operation.

There are of course further systems of control that can be used in a food and beverage operation but they become more and more complex as they try to measure areas of quality, performance and efficiency. Thus control can become a study in itself at a management level.

Here we shall look at the everyday controls that are used by the operatives and supervisors in our modern food and beverage operation. The key to successful control is the understanding that it is only a measuring system and once it has measured an activity it ceases to function. This is important as there can be a danger in the control activity becoming an obsessive activity in itself.

The two aspects of control mentioned above can be studied in relation to our operation under the headings of checking systems and billing systems.

Checking systems

There are three main reasons for having checking systems:

1 To make sure that everything issued is accounted for.
2 To make sure that all credit sales are paid for.
3 To guide us to the type of things that are popular and sell well.

Two types of checking system are in common use:

1 A la carte checking system which reflects a complex pricing structure.
2 Table d'hôte checking system used to quickly control a package deal.

The paperwork used in these two checking systems falls into one of the following categories:

1 Duplicate hand written checks.
2 Triplicate hand written checks.
3 Duplicate combined bill and strip check.
4 Pre-printed combined check and bill.
5 Machine print-out for mechanised and electronic systems.

It is important to realise that whilst there is a great variation in the methods used in each of these categories of paperwork, the fundamental principles of control remain the same. To put this very simply, we are concerned in knowing exactly what commodities are being consumed and by whom. This information requires to be recorded and checked for accuracy.

The first document that is used is the waiter's check.

The waiters' check

This is the starting point of any food service control system. If the system is to be effective there are a number of criteria that must be used to regulate the use of this document:

1 The waiter must use a check for every item he serves to a guest.
2 The check must be clearly written in either duplicate or triplicate.
3 The check must have an authorised signature.

NB the diagram shows the waiter's check that is used for food service with all its essential components.

These essential components are:

1 The table number
2 The number of guests
3 The date

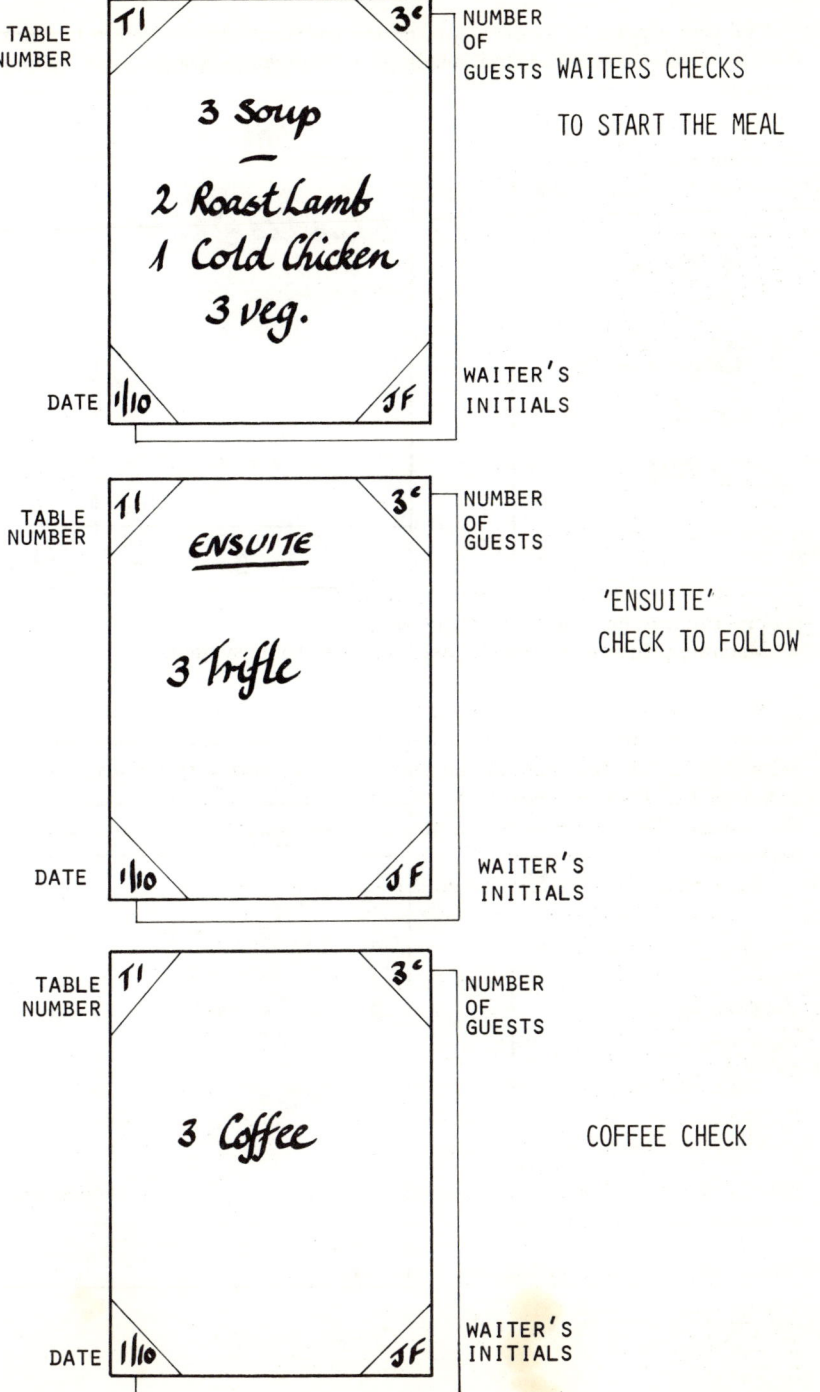

TABLE NUMBER — T1

NUMBER OF GUESTS — 3ᶜ

3 Soup
—
2 Roast Lamb
1 Cold Chicken
3 veg.

DATE — 1/10

WAITER'S INITIALS — JF

WAITERS CHECKS

TO START THE MEAL

TABLE NUMBER — T1

NUMBER OF GUESTS — 3ᶜ

ENSUITE

3 Trifle

DATE — 1/10

WAITER'S INITIALS — JF

'ENSUITE'
CHECK TO FOLLOW

TABLE NUMBER — T1

NUMBER OF GUESTS — 3ᶜ

3 Coffee

DATE — 1/10

WAITER'S INITIALS — JF

COFFEE CHECK

TABLE D'HÔTE CHECK AND BILL

RESTAURANT		£	P
DATE 1/10/81			
3 Lunches @ £3.50		10	50
SERVICE %			
V.A.T.			
	TOTAL		

TABLE	COVERS	WAITER	VAT.NO.
1	3	JF	12365

Check card shows:

T1   3ᶜ
3 Soup
—
2 Roast Lamb
1 Cold Chicken
3 veg.
1/10   JF

INCLUSIVE PRICE FOR THE FULL MEAL

À LA CARTE CHECK AND BILL

RESTAURANT		£	P
1/10/81			
3 Soup		1	20
2 Roast Lamb		5	00
1 Cold Chicken		2	00
3 Vegetables		1	50
3 Trifle			
3 Coffee			
SERVICE%			
V.A.T.			
	TOTAL		

TABLE	COVERS	WAITER	VAT.NO.
1	3	JF	12365

Check card shows:

T1   3ᶜ
3 Soup £1.20
2 Roast Lamb £5
1 Cold Chicken £2
3 veg. £1.50
1/10   JF

EACH ITEM PRICED SEPARATELY

4 The authorised signature or initials
5 The body of the check which contains:
  A Details of the guest's order
  B Quantity required
  C Sequence of service.

The purpose of the waiter's check

The waiter's original check is used to provide information to the supply department, usually the kitchen. For this reason it is important to give some advance information, and common practice is to tell the kitchen through this check not only of the guests immediate requirements, but also of the following course: thus a waiter's check is written in the first instance for the starter dish and also the main course.

Subsequent checks are used for additional items, such as sweet and coffee.

The check used by the wine waiter for beverages is no different from the food check in principle but a different colour is sometimes used to avoid confusion.

The dublicate or copy check is used to inform the cashier of the transaction that has been carried out by the food waiter and the wine waiter. This information should be identical to the information on the original check so that the correct amount of money can be collected for the food and beverages served.

Depending on whether there is an inclusive package charge or a detailed item pricing system. The waiter's check may or may not detail the charges to be made.

The guest's bill

This document is compiled from the information on the different food and wine checks that are submitted in respect of a guest or party of guests on any one occasion. The total bill may be settled immediately in cash by the casual guest or it may be charged to an account for a resident guest, regular guest or client who has made the arrangement to settle by account.

If the guest is not going to settle the bill immediately it is usual to collect the guest's signature on the bill as a means of temporary settlement and approval of the amount charged.

One of the problems that can arise from this billing system is that all items may not have been recorded. There requires to be careful supervision in a food service operation to ensure that charges are not omitted from a guest's bill.

Once the guest has settled his bill it is usual to provide him with a receipted copy. Thus we require to operate a duplicate billing system.

The billing system can be manual and written from the waiter's checks or it can be mechanised and printed with the information coming from the waiter's checks. Alternatively there are some systems where the waiter writes directly on the guest's bill. This type of system has the advantage of reducing the number of opportunities for error, but lacks the advantage of a kitchen check. Information on this system is given to the supply department verbally. The diagrams show the different forms of bill that can be used:

1 Manual separate bill.
2 Combined check and bill.
3 Waiter written bill.

To ensure an adequate control check on any of these systems it is necessary to retain the copy document for later comparison with the copy of the original check.

RESTAURANT				
M..........				
VAT REG NO.		DATE		
	COUVERT			
	CAFE			
	WINES			
	SPIRITS			
	CIGS			
TABLE	GUESTS	SERVICE%		
		V.A.T.		
101543		TOTAL £		

Manual Bill
This type of bill is prepared from the information on the different waiter's checks

A summary of all bills prepared is kept to provide an analysis of sales and expected revenue from cash and credit sales.

The preparation of bills and checks is something that should be practiced with care as carbon copy documents if carelessly written are of no use for control purposes.

Restaurant check control system (refer to flow diagram page 85)
The movement of paperwork in a check control system should be in a complete circle if control is to be effective. There are four basic areas of activity involved in the operation:

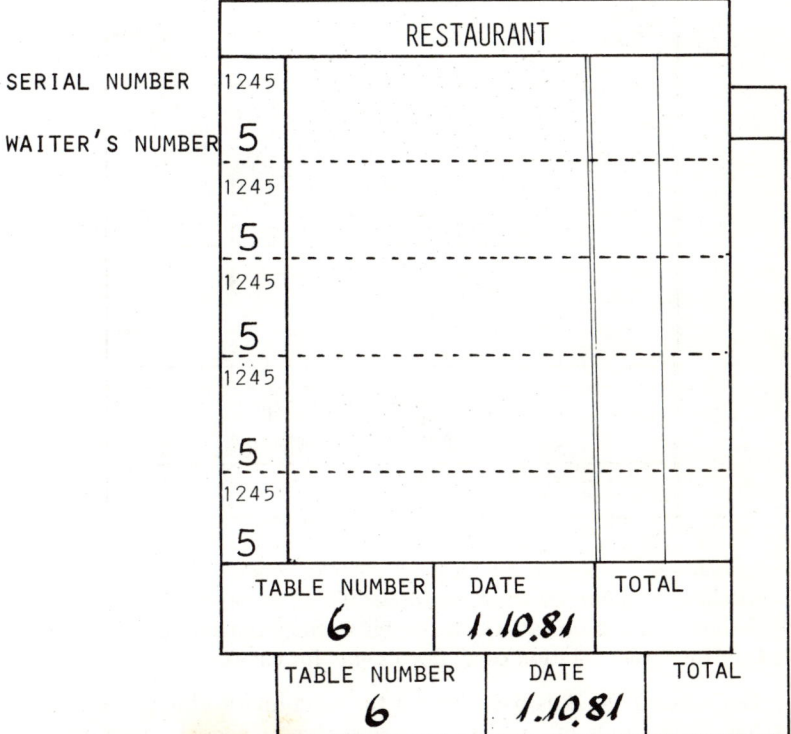

Combined checks and bill
The disadvantage of this type of bill is that it can be untidy if prepared by the waiter in haste

Machine printed bill or original bill prepared by waiter
As each item is served it is recorded directly on this type of bill by the
waiter using a machine thus the bill is ready (except for addition) at any
point during the meal. This system is ideal for a quick service operation.
The guest can either pay the waiter or take the bill to a cash desk on
the way out

RESTAURANT					
TABLE	COVERS	DATE	WAITER	£	P

FOOD

DRINKS

PLEASE PAY THE
AMOUNT SHOWN HERE

101543

1 Restaurant — source of original checks where service takes place.
2 Kitchen — point of issue of foodstuffs (can be bar for drinks, etc).
3 Cashier — the point at which the bill is prepared and money collected.
4 Control - the collation of all documents for checking.

The waiter's check is passed from the restaurant to the supply point in exchange for goods of equal value (no check = no goods). The copy check (which must be identical to original) should be passed to the cashier to show what goods have been supplied and to whom they have been supplied in order that an accurate bill can be prepared. Ultimately the documents or their copies are all passed to control so that they can be

The complete restaurant check control system
Bills with their original and copy checks all in agreement ▷

COMPLETE CHECK CONTROL SYSTEM

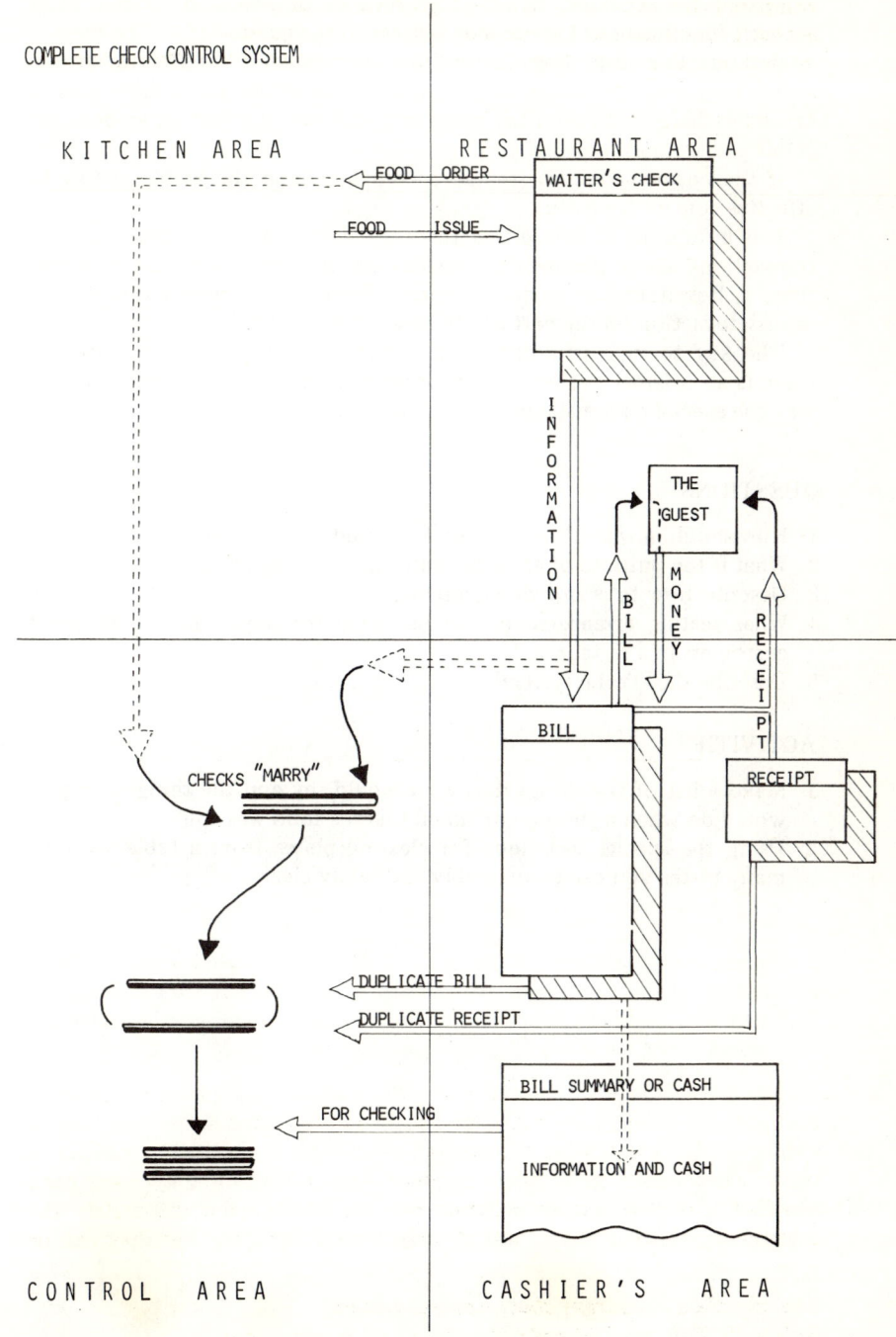

KITCHEN AREA   RESTAURANT AREA

FOOD ORDER

WAITER'S CHECK

FOOD ISSUE

INFORMATION

THE GUEST

BILL

MONEY

RECEIPT

BILL

RECEIPT

CHECKS "MARRY"

DUPLICATE BILL

DUPLICATE RECEIPT

BILL SUMMARY OR CASH

FOR CHECKING

INFORMATION AND CASH

CONTROL AREA   CASHIER'S AREA

compared for accuracy. In effect all revenue or potential revenue must account for all issues of goods and services to the guest.

Without this final stage of control the system is ineffective as the waiter may over- or under-charge. It is also possible for the cashier to over- or under-charge, and even the guest may not pay the correct amount for goods and services received.

If the entire system is seen as a complete loop the whole picture of effective control is evident.

It is important to realise that this system only takes account of normal transactions and supplementary checks are required for situations where there is hospitality or where the service breaks down with either default or dissatisfaction on the part of the guest.

The key to successful control at the operational stage is to insist that there is an original waiter's check for every single type of situation. In this way the special circumstances can be dealt with.

QUESTIONS

1 How should a waiter's service cloth be used during silver service?
2 What is the purpose of an underplate when serving soup?
3 Describe how to crumb down a table.
4 What seating arrangements can be made for physically handicapped customers in a restaurant?
5 Describe the 'Tronc system'.

ACTIVITIES

1 Make a list of the things that your would say and the things that you would do when a guest complained that his food was cold.
2 Using the special technique for clearing plates from a table see how many plates you can comfortably and safely clear.

6
Salesmanship

Sales and service — procedure for meeting and seating guests
Meet, greet and seat guests in that order.

Meeting the guests is normally the responsibility of the restaurant manager/ess, headwaiter/ess, or whoever is the person in charge. The activity begins in the reception area, where at the reception desk the reservation book is checked and tables are allocated. It is here that a good first impression is created with a smile of welcome, and a courteous manner, and where it is very important to make a point of remembering and addressing regular patrons by name. A good memory is an invaluable asset in the hospitality industry. The reception area should always be under surveillance and guests should never be left to stand around unattended and perhaps wander into the dining area searching for a table.

The guests should be politely escorted to their table and there be handed over to the station headwaiter or station waiter (depending on the staffing arrangements). At the table the waiter will, after a pleasant greeting, proceed to seat the party. If ladies are present they will be seated first: despite changing attitudes on sexual equality, attentive waiting staff should always treat ladies with an 'olde worlde' courtesy. This is important with regard to the professional business woman travelling alone, who spends a great deal of her time in restaurants. She is very sensitive to atmosphere, and will appreciate receiving the same consideration and attention enjoyed by male diners and larger parties.

When guests are comfortably seated, they will be presented with the menus, from the left, and while they are discussing and deciding on the meal, the waiter will occupy himself with small duties. These will include such tasks as placing butter on the table, offering rolls, etc. at the same time the waiter must be alert for the moment when the party are ready to order.

The well trained waiter will know the menu thoroughly. He will be able to describe the composition of any dish and, if asked, he will also be aware of the preparation time of the main dish and any à la carte items.

If his help is sought in the ordering of the meal he will be able to offer suggestions, describing attractively the merits of the various dishes. He will organise the taking of the order to be read and clearly understood so that the right dishes go to the guests who ordered them.

After the food order has been taken. The wine waiter will approach and ask if the guests wish to see the wine list. If the guests do not want wine, soft drinks can be offered. It is important for the wine waiter to be able to advise the guests on their choice of a suitable drink. This is where he will use his expertise and talent in salesmanship in advising on the selection of aperitifs, wines, liqueurs, etc.

By this time the first course should appear and the meal progress with no delays, in a smooth operation, which will make the guests feel relaxed and confident that their welfare is in capable hands.

The food and beverage staff should make a point of identifying the host of the party.

It will be noted that the technique of salesmanship involves all members of the food and beverage service staff.

Merchandising and sales

Salesmanship is such an integral part of a food and beverage operation that a philosophy of selling must influence and activate all policies. Restaurant/dining-room selling is non-aggressive calm and polite. The menu has to be planned, not just as a list of items, but as an advertising and a promotional agent. It must be clean, attractive and up-to-date.

Popular profitable dishes such as salads, appetisers and desserts should be well publicised and temptingly described. House specialities can be highlighted to catch the eye of the customer. The overall presentation will reflect the thought and care which has been taken in the compilation of the menu.

The primary selling aid of the food and beverage staff is the menu. It not only sells food. It sells the establishment as well.

Guests who ask for a menu as a souvenir should never be refused, it is an effective means of advertising at low cost, and a compliment to the management. If the menu is expensive to produce and there is a problem of cost when giving guests menus as souvenirs, it is a useful advertising technique, to have small replica menus produced that can be readily given away to guests as they are leaving.

Keen progressive staff are an invaluable asset, and should be encouraged to use their intelligence by incorporating such adjectives as savoury, succulent, fragrant, aromatic and featherlight, into their vocabulary when explaining and describing menu items which are to be highly recommended to the guests.

Making suggestions means recommending food, beverage, and services which will enhance the meal for the diner and also benefit the staff and the establishment through increased sales and gratutities.

Tactful suggestions for cocktails, aperitifs and appetisers, while waiting for a dish cooked to order; helpful ideas for extras such as garlic bread, vegetables, special sauces, etc, are all good sales techniques.

Desserts are profitable but not always easy to sell to calorie conscious guests, nevertheless an attractive tempting display of desserts on a sweet trolley often proves very hard for the guest to resist.

The inclusion of a display of fine cheeses can add a gourmet touch to a restaurant and encourage extra wine sales.

A major factor in building and maintaining a reputation is the absolute cleanliness of the establishment. Customers may not always complain to the management about careless standards, they will just tell their friends, and do not come back. This is one area where there should never be any cause for dissatisfaction. Guests must be surrounded by sparkling cleanliness in every aspect of the operation.

The most effective advertising costs nothing more than a little effort on the part of all staff. It is the testimony of satisfied customers who build up goodwill by spreading the word of the excellence of an establishment.

Complementary to the menu as a sales aid is the wine list. Many wine lists are unfortunately dull and unimaginative, with page after page of specialist terms often only understood by the wine expert. A good wine list should be as attractive as a good menu and eye-catching, with a selection to suit most tastes and pockets.

The merchandising of liquor and cigars can be done with style and flair by the wine waiter (sommelier). He must be discreet in his suggestions, but stylish in his presentation.

The wine list need not have any restrictions, and can be as informative as the management wish it to be. It should make interesting reading with perhaps some historical detail and drawings to catch and hold the customers' attention.

A promotional feature with a continuous theme could be, 'the wine of the day' chosen to complement the 'dish of the day', with a special tariff. An added attraction could be a paragraph on the menu with a potted history of the origin and region of this wine. The food menu could have a similar theme.

Most wine and spirit bottles have attractive labels and shapes which would show to advantage, placed in strategic positions in the dining area. These could be highlighted to show off the jewel-like colours of the glass and subtly suggest the idea of beverages to the diner.

A sparkling clean trolley, laid up with liqueurs and brandies and the soft glow of the wood and gold decoration of cigar boxes can be irresistible in encouraging the diner to indulge in an after dinner brandy or liquer, particularly when it is readily available and attractively displayed before him. The opportunity is there to be selective and perhaps a little adventurous in trying out a hitherto unfamiliar drink.

A final point that the wine waiter must remember is to avoid being too clever when asked for information or help. Tact is the watchword. The knowledgeable guest will resent being talked down to, and the novice guest will feel uncomfortable if made to appear inexperienced. The wine waiter must be an expert judge of human nature and develop the skill and experience of handling all types of guests with tact and diplomacy.

Profitability has to be achieved to stay in business. Therefore everyone must endeavour to activate and stimulate sales in each operational area.

Food service staff can promote food sales with tactful attractive descriptions of menu items.

Beverage staff could have eye-catching displays of wines, liqueurs and cigars displayed on trolleys or in cabinets.

Management and supervisory staff have the responsibility of achieving results through the work of others by evaluating and utilising personnel productively by reducing waste, by instigating change to promote growth, by disciplined leadership in creating an atmosphere of respect and dignity in regard to the importance of every member of the team. It is essential to maintain a spirit of mutual co-operation. Any manager can issue orders, but it takes a good manager to motivate the staff, by recognising and appreciating their talents and their contribution to the operation. His ability to communicate with them will stem from his own training and understanding, and knowledge of every aspect of the food and beverage service. With good leadership, employees will be inspired with a sense of pride and identity and this atmosphere will be conveyed to the customer, who will be in a more receptive mood for the promotion of extra sales. The manager is the person who will always get that little bit of extra effort from his staff when it is needed.

Good profits and successful image depend on satisfied customers. The quality which can distinguish one operation from another, comes from the concern for the customers' comfort and well-being. This concern is an element which has to be developed by intelligent management and fostered in employees as part of their training and personal pride in the organisation.

Too many people are ready to dismiss yesterday's standards as old-fashioned. There is nothing old-fashioned about the 'spirit of service' — that will never go out of style. Many of the former standards can and should be used with good effect today, otherwise there is little or no judgement for excellence. Many operations never rise above the level of their own mediocrity.

It is said that success has its own criteria, but this does not always equate with satisfaction, in staff, management, or customer. This age of speed, fast food and fast travel encourages impersonal attitudes. Every small personal service can pay dividends in promotion and job satisfaction. Helping a mother with young children by supplying high chairs and bibs is an aspect of personal service.

Changing a dish without argument gives an impression of well-mannered staff; paying particular attention to the lone diner by being alert to his attempts to attract attention; a friendly helpful approach towards the elderly or foreign visitor, all indicate an enterprise which cares about people. The food and beverage service industry is essentially about people.

Guéridon service (side table service)

This service requires professional skill and a certain flair for showmanship. It is a form of entertainment, but more important it helps to promote sales.

The guéridon can be used for the service of a complete meal or for the preparation of a speciality dish. Where a dish is cooked at the guéridon the customer can indicate the method and degree of cooking that he prefers. In all cases of guéridon preparation it is essential for the waiter to have a good knowledge of the preparation of food as well as its service.

When serving soup from a tureen or preparing starters such as prawn or fruit cocktails, the guéridon can be used so that the customer is more involved in the intricacies of service. Salads can be prepared with their individual dressings to the guest's particular taste. Fish dishes can be filleted and meat carved to order. Poultry and game can be portioned as can various meats and pies. The speciality coffees that are offered can be prepared at the guéridon. The complete preparation and cooking of a main dish or special sweet can be carried out in front of the customer. Several classic favourites are prepared in this way, such as Steak Diane or Crêpes Suzettes.

The customer enjoys a feeling of participation and anticipation, whilst watching the food being taken through the various stages of its preparation. This public display of food preparation is quite common in luxury restaurants in Europe and is a speciality of Japanese restaurants.

A guéridon is a side table which is slightly higher than a normal restaurant table and fairly small with sufficient space to perform the tasks described above. In order that it can be readily moved around the restaurant it normally has two or four wheels.

For cooking, a flare lamp can be additional or incorporated into the guéridon. This lamp is normally fuelled by methylated spirits or butane gas. The modern guéridon trolley is equipped with a built in lamp and has a separate gas container so that refuelling is not required freqently. There is normally a cutlery drawer and lower shelf for equipment and bottles. An adjustable shelf extension can also be incorporated. The main purpose of the guéridon is to allow the waiter to carry out sideboard activities at the guests' table, by bringing the dishes and equipment into view of the guests during service. The guéridon trolley allows the waiter to withdraw from the guests' table after he has performed the preparation and presentation, so that he may then go to another table for the same purpose.

Steak Diane
Mise-en Place
Flattened fillet steak. Worcester sauce, finely chopped onion, diced mushrooms, butter, salt and pepper mill, fresh cream, cognac, chafing pan and flare lamp, service spoons and forks, hot plates.
Method
1 Season the steak with salt and pepper while the butter is melting in the chafing pan.
2 Place the steak into the pan and cook lightly on both sides.
3 Remove the steak and keep hot between two hot plates while the sauce is being prepared.
4 Fry off the chopped onions in the butter and as they begin to colour add the diced mushrooms.
5 Return the steak to the pan and season with a sprinkle of Worcester sauce.
6 Flame with Cognac, adding cream, and then serve on to a hot plate.

Preparation of steak diane

Seasoning the steaks

Cooking the steaks

Adding onions and mushrooms

Cooking onions and mushrooms

Flame with Cognac

Adding cream

Crêpes Suzettes
Mise-en-place
Cooked wafer thin pancakes, butter, lemon and orange juice in sauce boats, caster sugar, sugar lumps impregnated with orange and lemon, orange curacao, cognac, flare lamp, crêpe pan, service spoons and forks, hot plates.

Method

1　Place a tablespoon of caster sugar in the crêpe pan.
2　As the sugar begins to caramelise add some butter and mix well.
3　Add some orange and lemon juice.
4　Dissolve the sugar lumps in the sauce.
5　Add the curacao to flavour the sauce and give a smooth consistency.
6　Place a crêpe flat in the pan and wash over with sauce.
7　Turn the crêpe, sprinkle with sugar and fold into a triangular shape.
8　Place this crêpe to one side of the pan and repeat with the others.
9　The sauce should be kept fluid with lemon and orange juice while all the requisite crêpes are prepared.
10　Finally sprinkle caster sugar over the crêpes and flame by adding cognac.
11　Serve crêpes on to hot plates while still flaming.

NB　Always add liquor from a sauce boat and never directly from the bottle.

Plat du jour trolley

This trolley is used for presenting the 'plat du jour' or 'dish of the day', which can be a joint of roast beef, lamb or pork, or a whole turkey. The meats are carved and served to the diner at the table in the restaurant.

The trolley is completely mobile for ease of movement between tables. The top section of the trolley is a silver plated hinged dome which swings open to reveal the carving surface. When the trolley is in use, the dome swings neatly round underneath the lower half.

The dish of the day rests on a carving board placed over a water container which is kept hot be two spirit lamps. A plate rest extends from the top of the trolley to hold the heated plates in readiness for the portion of carved meat. Containers of sauce or gravy are next to the carving board. One or two shelves below are used for holding hot plates and service cutlery.

The size of the restaurant would decide whether or not trolleys such as this could be used, as they tend to be space consuming. However, the plat du jour trolley is a good sales aid and can be used in conjunction with other trolleys to give an elegant touch to a restaurant.

If the customer can see some of the food offered on display, sales can be greatly promoted. Trolleys are often used for hors d'oeuvres, salads, sweets, cheeses and liqueurs and can extend the range of guéridon service.

QUESTIONS

1　What are the first five activities that take place when a guest arrives in a restaurant?
2　How can the menu be used to promote sales?

Preparation of crêpes suzettes

Melting sugar

Blend in juice

Add flavoured cubes

Add liqueur

Lift up crêpe

Place crêpe in sauce

Sprinkle with sugar

Flame with brandy

3　In what ways can beverages be displayed?
4　Give two examples of personal service to a customer.
5　What is the purpose of restaurant check control?

ACTIVITIES

1　Collect a number of wine lists and menus and compare their sales promotion qualities.
2　Devise a simple system of controlling food service without the writing of checks or bills.

7
Beverage Service

Part I — Glasses and Wine and Bar Service

The correct handling of glasses is very important because of the high cost of replacements and the danger of accidents and injuries.

Breakages must be kept to a minimum. When glasses are collected this should be done very carefully by handling the base or stem of the glass and never placing fingers inside the bowl.

Ideally glasses should be washed and rinsed separately in clean hot water, with a bacteriacidal detergent or rinsing agent. The glasses must be thoroughly rinsed to remove all traces of detergent or soap, as any residue would discolour the glass and taint the contents. Ideally a glass washing machine should be used where the temperature and quantity of detergent are carefully controlled, and all glasses should be inspected after washing.

When drying or polishing glasses by hand a lint free linen glass cloth should be used and the glasses dried immediately after they have been rinsed and drained, before they cool.

Technique for drying and polishing glasses
To dry or polish the glass, first of all stuff the end of the drying cloth into the bowl of the glass and rotate the glass whilst drying and polishing the outside of the glass with the rest of the cloth.

Never polish or dry the glass with fingers inside the bowl and always make sure that the part of the hand between thumb and fingers is well protected by the cloth. Even the slightest chip or crack can cause severe injury to the hand.

Once the glasses have been polished they should be stored so that they do not gather dust, by either storing upside down, or in an upright position with clean paper or cloths over the top of the bowls.

Sizes and shapes of glasses
The various sizes and shapes of all glasses are too numerous to mention, and can readily be studied in manufacturers catalogues. For general use however, the following range would suit most purposes. Perhaps the most versatile glass of all is the *Paris goblet* which can be used for wines, spirits, sparkling drinks, etc. The sizes available vary from a small size suitable for sherry to a very large size that can be used for lager.

There are a number of manufacturers variations on the Paris goblet with similar ranges of sizes, such as the *Crown goblet* or the *Barmaster*, where the shape is different but the purpose similar. A perfect glass should be thin and clear so that the contents can be appreciated. There should be a stem so that the hand does not heat the contents of the glass, and the bowl should be sufficiently large to allow the contents to be swirled to release the bouquet of wines in particular. The glass should curve gently inwards towards the rim to retain such a bouquet, but should still be shaped so that it can be easily cleaned.

A glass should be filled to about two thirds of its capacity and never to the brim.

Too large a glass distorts the bouquet and too small a glass prevents it being enjoyed.

The quality of glasses will be determined by the standard of the restaurant and the amount of money available. Breakages will occur in any operation from time to time and to obtain a glass that has unbreakable qualities the standard inevitably suffers.

Some luxury restaurants will go to the other extreme and use crystal glasses, which, whilst very elegant, are not entirely practical, being very expensive and difficult to clean.

Special glasses for wines

The Paris goblet or its equivalent is ideal for table wines. Fine wines like claret and burgundy should be served in a glass with a generously sized bulb shaped bowl, which curves inward to retain the bouquet. Such wines are served to only half fill the glass.

German wines such as hocks and moselles are traditionally served in

Types of glasses

Name of glass	Approximate Capacity	Design
Champagne	5 fl oz (15cl)	Tulip or saucer
Burgandy	8 fl oz (24cl)	Stemmed bulb shape
Bordeaux	6 fl oz (18cl)	Stemmed bulb shape
Rhine wine (Hock)	6 fl oz (18cl)	Long amber stemmed
Moselle (Mosel)	6 fl oz (18cl)	Long green stemmed
Sherry (Copita)	4 fl oz (12cl)	Small tulip shape
Port	4 fl oz (12cl)	Small bell shaped
Liquer	2 fl oz (6cl)	Small thistle shape
Cocktail	3 fl oz (9cl)	Various shallow bowls
Brandy	5 fl oz (15cl)	Balloon shaped
Beer	10-20 fl oz (30-60cl)	Tumblers/Tankards

Note
With the exception of beers the glasses are filled to half or three quarters of their capacity and not to the brim.

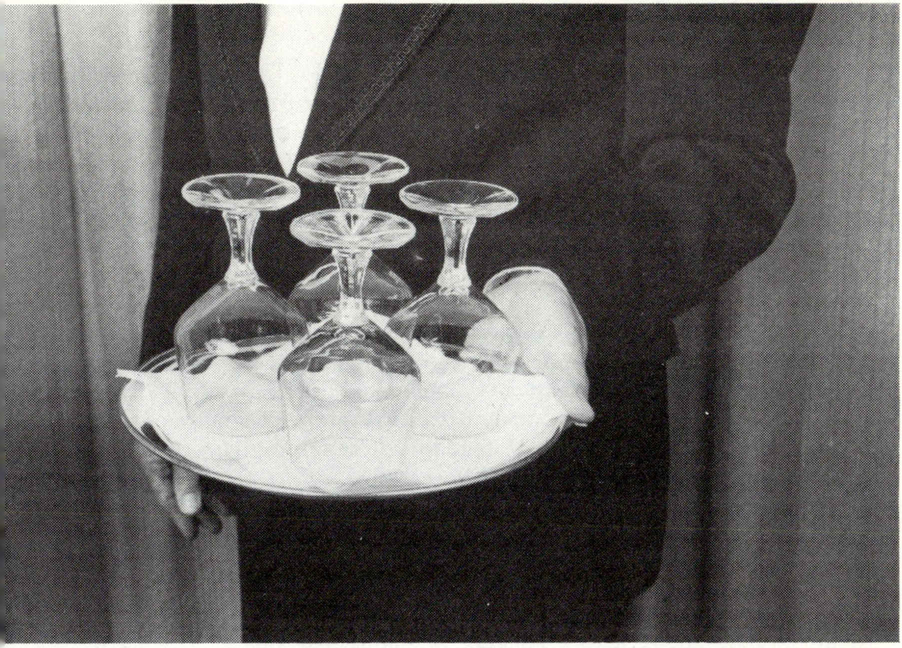

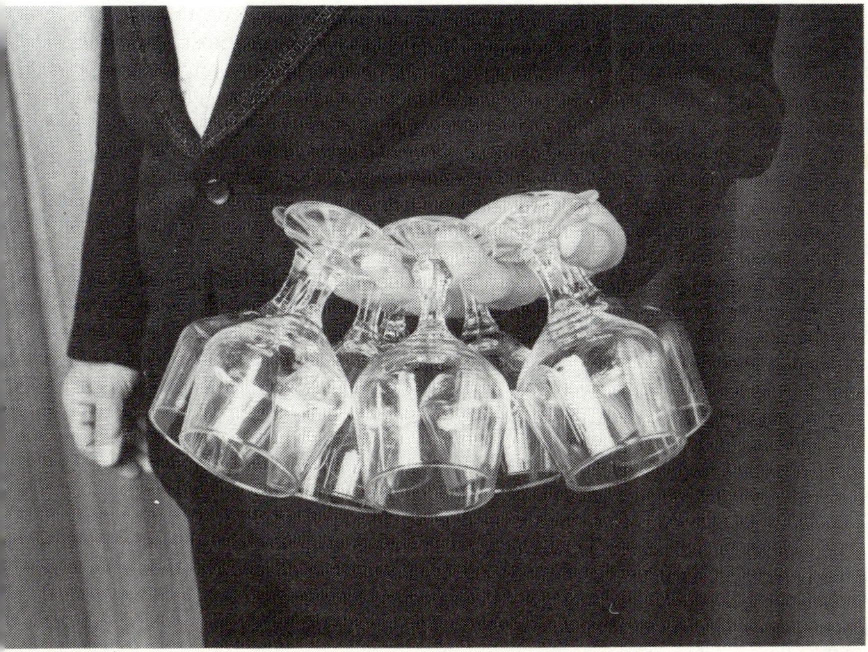

very tall stemmed glasses with small round bowls. The stem of the glass should match the colour of the bottle, with the bowl usually clear.

Champagne is popularly served in shallow saucer shaped glasses but a much more suitable glass is the tall tulip shape which holds and allows a steady rise of bubbles.

After-dinner drinks such as brandy and port have their own special glasses too. Balloon shaped glasses for brandy, which should be easily held in the hand so that the liqueur can be swirled around and the bouquet savoured.

Port is served in small glasses which are often cut glass or crystal to match the decanter used for service.

Each type of wine, particularly French wine, has its own style of glass, but it is not practical for a restaurant to carry too wide a range of shapes and sizes. It is better to have a standard multi-purpose glass and a few glasses for special drinks or for special occasions.

If serving a house wine by the glass, the size chosen would relate to the amount of wine being sold by the glass at any given price.

Pre-meal drinks

Many establishments have a cocktail or lounge bar adjacent to the restaurant where guests can enjoy a leisurely drink while waiting for a table. Very often they can order their meal and wine in advance while having an aperitif.

The person in charge of the bar usually dispenses and serves drinks to guests at the bar or lounge tables. He can also be responsible for the dispensing of wines and all drinks to the restaurant, although the actual serving will be carried out by the sommelier. If there is no cocktail or lounge bar, the sommelier will ask if pre-meal drinks are required, once the guests are seated at their table. These would then be dispensed from a dispense bar usually situated behind the scenes. This supply bar normally services a number of outlets in an establishment including restaurants, lounges, function rooms and floor service.

The person in charge of this bar has to be fully experienced in stock control and the dispensing of all kinds of drinks. In addition it is essential that he has a knowledge of all the various wines offered on the wine list.

The dispense bar may have a small counter or hatch and will be positioned for easy access to facilitate the service to the different areas.

Ample stocks have to be carried which necessitates a large area for storage. All wines are stored in numbered bins to correspond with the numbers on the wine list. Red wines are kept at a constant room temperature and white wines are stored chilled.

All orders are only dispensed to wine service staff on receipt of a properly documented check which is either duplicate or triplicate, and carries the following details: table or room number, bin number (wines), required drinks priced, date and signature. There are no cash transactions in the dispense bar.

Champagne Tulip

Champagne Saucer

Bordeaux/Burgundy

Rhine or Mosel

Sherry

Port

Liqueur

Brandy

Cocktail

Service of table wines

When the sommelier (wine waiter) makes his first approach to a guest it should be in a friendly manner with a polite greeting. He will ask if aperitifs are required and offer the wine list or special drinks list to the host of the party, from the right. He may be called upon to offer some advice on the merits of different cocktails, sherries or spirits.

The first order must be carried out very quickly so that there is no delay in the meal service.

Once the guests have ordered their food the wine order should be taken as soon as possible so that the first wine, if it is a white wine, can be ready on ice, waiting by the table. This is important when there is a large party and more than one wine is being served. The sommelier will stand to the right of the host when presenting the bottle, with the label uppermost so that the host can confirm that it is as ordered. This is most important before the wine is opened, and it also provides the host with an opportunity to change his mind or to reject a wine before it is too late.

Red wines with a few exceptions should be served at room temperature (Chambre); Bordeaux wines 64°F (18°C) slightly warmer than Burgundy, 60°F (16°C). As these wines are generally stored at a lower temperature in cellar conditions a good restaurant will have a small stock of wines ready for service in a cabinet of storage area, near to the restaurant, around room temperature.

White wines can be kept slightly refrigerated. It is important that wine should not be subjected to sudden changes of temperature.

Once the guest's wine has been presented and accepted it can be opened. To open the bottle, the capsule covering the cork should be removed by cutting around the top lip of the bottle. The capsule may be foil or plastic and should be cut cleanly so that it is removed away from the top lip. It should never be torn off. The top of the bottle and cork should now be wiped clean.

There are a variety of corkscrews that can be used to open a bottle of wine, and it is important that the wine waiter uses a good corkscrew that will not split the cork. Ideally a waiter's 'comfort' or combined corkscrew, knife and bottle opener is used as the knife blade can be used for removing the capsule.

The point of the corkscrew is inserted into the top of the cork at a slight angle so that it will penetrate the cork. It is then straightened up before it is screwed down. The corkscrew is inserted until only one spiral of the screw is visible. Do not insert it too far or the bottom of the cork will break. Corks do vary in length and practice and experience will lead to mastering the technique. The cork should now be gently eased from the bottle. This is made very easy when using the waiter's 'comfort', as there is a lever that can be clamped on the top edge of the neck. Some other devices have a similar lever. If the corkscrew does not have such a lever it is more difficult to remove the cork and the bottle must not be placed between the knees and the corkscrew be given a mighty tug. The cork should not be allowed to 'pop' out suddenly.

Wine Service

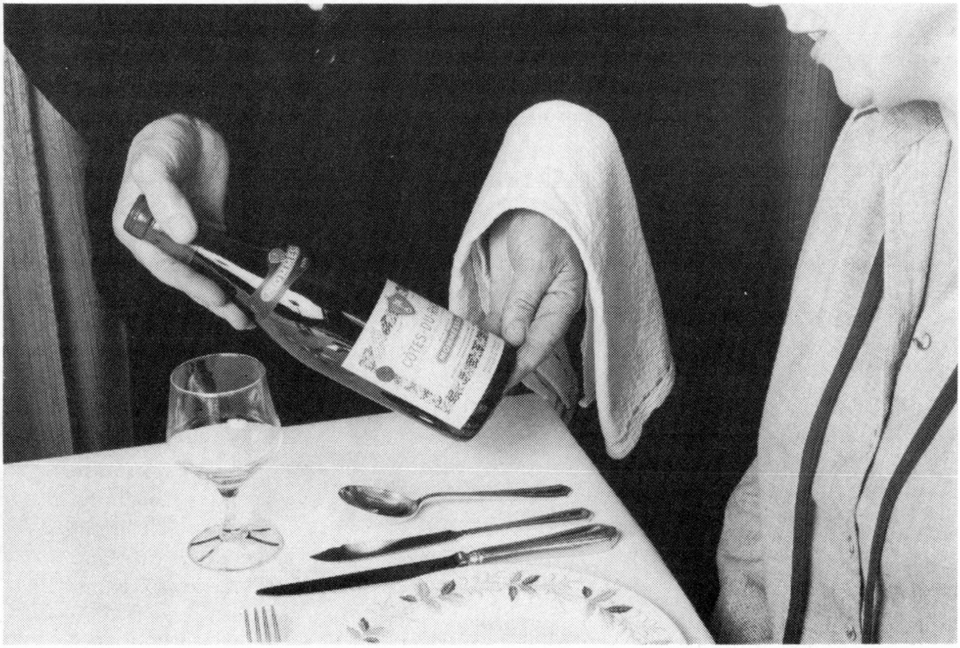

Presenting the bottle

Inserting the corkscrew

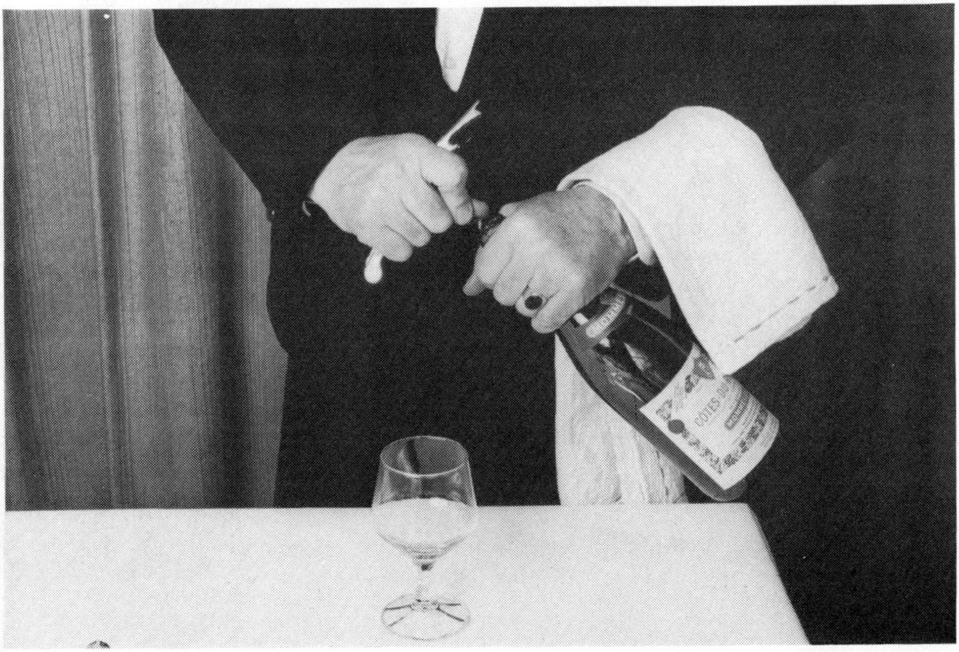

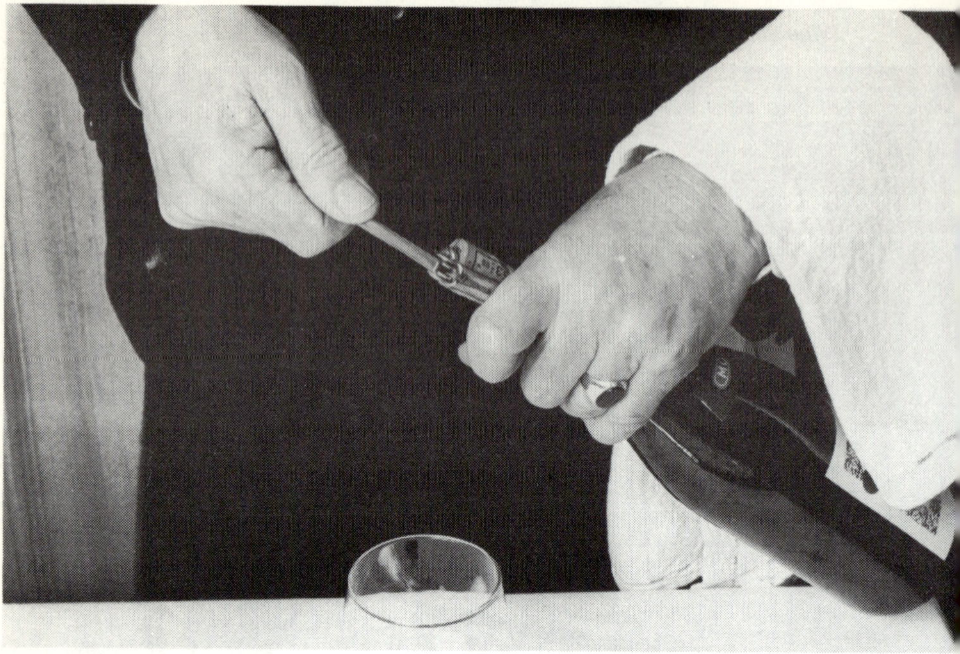

Drawing the cork

Pouring wine for tasting

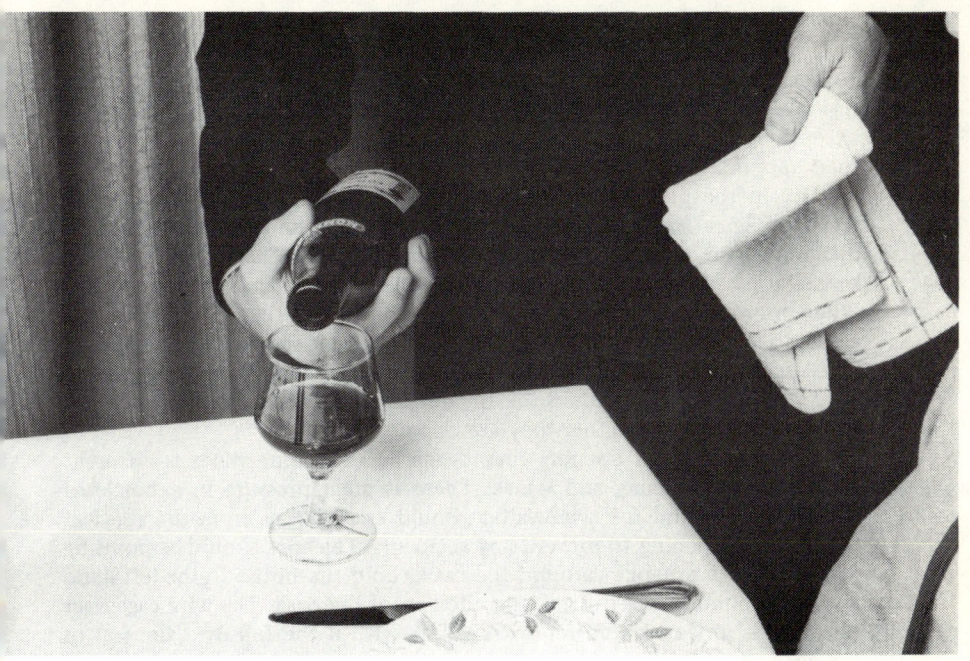

Half turning the bottle to prevent dripping

Once the cork has been removed the neck of the bottle should be wiped clean and the cork retained for inspection if required. Red wines are generally opened early and left for a while to 'breathe', allowing the air to come into contact with the wine.

A small quantity of wine is poured into the host's glass so that it can be tasted. The host will judge the wine for colour, bouquet, temperature and taste, and normally accept the wine unless there is something wrong with it. Once the wine has been approved it is served to the other guests on the host's right, working in an anti-clockwise direction, serving ladies first. The host is last to have his wine served.

Pour the wine into the glass and, after stopping the flow, give the bottle a quick twist or half turn before drawing away from the glass. This technique will prevent the last drop of wine from dripping on to the table cloth. Once all the guests have been served with wine, the bottle is left in sight of the host. A white wine would be replaced in a wine cooler on a side table or stand, a red wine left on the table in a wine basket or on a wine coaster.

As the guests drink their wine the winewaiter should be attentive and top up the glasses so that they remain just over half full. When the wine is finished the waiter should see that the empty bottle is not removed before the host is aware that it has been finished.

Should the wine be unacceptable to the host after tasting, the bottle along with the cork which has been retained are returned and an alternative wine offered to the guest.

109

The sommelier, if asked, can from his own knowledge recommend a suitable wine in relation to the dish it will accompany, but there are exceptions to this rule. Guests do order and enjoy wines irrespective of their rapport with the meal ordered. A popular guide to wine and food affinity in the past was 'red wine with red meat' and 'white wine with fish' but since there are so many different wines and tastes within each different type of wine it is impossible to generalise. The customer is free to make his own choice and need not be bound by any of these rules. When more than one wine is served at a meal the first glass should be removed as soon as possible after the second wine is served.

Glasses must be taken away on a tray and handled by the base or stem only. On no account should the fingers be placed inside the bowl of the glasses to lift them, whether they are clean or dirty.

The technique for opening champagne and sparkling wines is different from that for opening still wines. There is great pressure in a bottle of sparkling wine and the winewaiter should stand away from the guest at the point of opening to prevent any accidents. The cork should be pointing upwards. With a napkin around the neck, hold the bottle in the left hand with the thumb pressed firmly on the top of the cork. The wire cage over the cork is unwound and removed taking with it the foil over the top of the cork.

The bottle is held at an angle and the cork is gently twisted out with the hand held firmly over it at all times. Once the cork has been eased it will come out without difficulty. The bottle can now be held upright and the napkin will absorb any foam which may bubble over. The neck should be wiped and any extra foil removed.

Sparkling wines are served as other table wines but when pouring care must be taken not to pour too quickly, especially in tall narrow glasses, as the wine foams and rises up the glass very quickly. The technique of pouring a sparkling wine is to pour a little into the glass at first and then allow the foam to subside before adding more, this way the wine will not foam up and out of the glass.

Outage

It is important when serving wines and other drinks in the restaurant to understand the quantities of liquids and the capacity of measures that are being handled. A simple example of this might be where a party of six guests order a bottle of wine and the wine waiter, after having allowed the host to taste the wine, pours over generous measures in each glass. The disastrous result can be that when he returns to top up the host's glass, he finds that there is insufficient wine left in the bottle.

A good general guide for serving table wine from standard bottles is to allow five glasses per bottle of wine. This guide however is not particularly accurate and cannot be used by the inexperienced. The simplest and perhaps most accurate method of ascertaining the number of glasses per bottle (outage) is to actually take a bottle of standard size and the

glass in common usage and practice pouring out the liquid to an acceptable level in the glass. This can be practised without wasting the real
liquor using water in an old bottle. Considerable difference in results will
be noticed if the glasses are over-filled.

Most wine today for restaurant use is supplied in bottles of 75 cl
capacity, but some may only be 70 cl and others litre size. A magnum
contains the equivalent of two standard bottles.

It should also be noted that some old fine wines contain a great deal
of sediment and therefore render a lower outage as a substantial amount
of residue has to be left in the bottle after pouring or decanting.

The difficulty in ascertaining a usual outage figure is not experienced
with spirits and liqueurs as they are normally measured in a fixed measure
before being poured into the glass, or are poured into a glass with a
graduation mark on it.

The term *five out* means five measures from a 'gill' or quarter of an
imperial pint is equivalent to 1 fluid ounce (approximately 3 cl).

Cocktail bars

A bar in an hotel or restaurant complex is part of the service to the
customer and makes a lucrative contribution to the profits. The overheads
are less than the restaurant or dining-room but ideas should always be
explored for promoting increased sales. The popularity of the Cocktail Bar,
or 'American Bar' and was its height during the 'Roaring Twenties' in
America, in London. The section of society known as 'The Bright Young
Things' made the cocktail fashionable.

The Second World War to a large extent saw the demise of the cocktail
habit due to the shortage of essential ingredients and expert bartenders.
The cocktail has never really regained the popularity it once enjoyed, as
the majority of the public tend to prefer bars where a variety of drinks,
from a glass of beer to some weird and wonderful concoctions can be
obtained, recent years have seen the growing popularity with young people
of bars where 'real ale' from the wood can be obtained, and along with the
growth of fast food outlets and American style dinners, the cocktail is
beginning to return.

An attractively designed smart cocktail bar, clean and comfortable,
under the control of an adept courteous bartender, skilled in the art
of mixing and dispensing an excellent cocktail with dexterity and style, is
a profitable asset in a food and beverage service operation.

Bars, whether cocktail or general must be well planned and well
organised. The restrictions imposed in a confined space necessitate
complete orderliness. There has to be a place for everything and everything
must be kept in its place. Storage cupboards and shelves have to be designed
for easy access to bottles and equipment. The height of the bar counter
should be comfortable, to suit the average customer.

The counter should also be at a convenient height for the bartender
to work. The top of the counter should be covered in a material easily

cleaned and hard wearing. The preparation of the ingredients for mixed drinks is done on the work bench underneath the bar counter. This under-counter can incorporate one or two stainless steel sinks with hot and cold running water, (a separate basin for handwashing is compulsory) and a draining area for glasses. A glasswashing machine is a useful addition. Adequate shelving is required for the storage of bottles to facilitate fast smooth service. The drinks must be mixed in full view of the customer so that he can appreciate the different skills of mixing, pouring and shaking. For safety non-slip durable flooring should cover the bar floor, which must be kept clear of empty bottles and debris. There should be a receptacle for containing these items.

A good supply of ice is essential and an ice-making machine is most useful, but refrigerated cupboards and shelves for the storage and chilling of certain items such as minerals, lagers, wines, etc, are a necessity.

The gantry (display shelves) behind the bar should be kept well stocked with a selection of good quality spirits and liqueurs. It is statutory for licensed premises to display prominently a list of prices of all drinks and the measures used for spirits: whisky, rum, gin and vodka.

Bar service is counter service on view to the customer who is aware of every phase of the operation, therefore strick rules of sanitation and hygiene must be observed.

Great care must be taken when handling glasses, utensils and garnishes for drinks. The bartender's hands and nails must be thoroughly clean and the uniform spotless.

Smoking behind a bar is forbidden by law. Staff should be made fully aware of this. The ice used in drinks must be lifted with tongs and not with bare hands. Ashtrays should be emptied into fireproof containers and washed separately from glasses. Bar cloths should be thoroughly rinsed out at the end of each day with a bacteriacidal detergent. Glass cloths must not be used for wiping down the bar counter, and should be laundered daily.

The equipment should always be ready to hand for successful bar-tending and will normally include: cocktail shaker, glass mixing jug, long handled mixing spoons, measures, ice tongs, fork for fruits, corkscrew, bottle opener, hawthorn strainer, cocktail sticks and straws, a fruit board and knife, insulated ice bucket, fresh clean ice, a selection of garnishes: pearl onions, olives, cherries, lemons, oranges, etc and a selection of bitters, gomme syrup and caster sugar.

It is essential that a responsible and knowledgeable person should be in charge of a bar of this type or any licensed premises.

Regardless of expensive décor and stylish surroundings, a bartender whose deportment is less than exemplary will not contribute to its success. Personality, combined with salesmanship and flair, discretion and tact, are the attributes for attracting and maintaining a clientele. The bartender must strive to be 'all things to all men' yet keep his distance, he can be friendly, without being over familiar. He is the recipient of many confidences, which must never be divulged. He can have a discussion, but never an argument, with a customer. The subjects of religion and politics are considered to be taboo. He should have a knowledge of general subjects and current topics. It can take years of training to become a competent head bartender and for that reason he/she is generally considered to be part of the management structure of the establishment.

It is not expected that the bartenders should know the composition of every cocktail or mixed drink but a knowledge of the most popular classics which have stood the test of time is indispensable. A few points on the mixing of cocktails:

1 Always use clean ice for each drink and place in the shaker or mixing glass first.
2 Never fill a shaker more than half full.
3 A short sharp shake for cocktails; don't allow the ice to melt and dilute the drink.
4 Glasses should be chilled.
5 The drinks should be attractive and appeal to the eye as well as the palate.
6 Never use a shaker when a recipe says mix; the result will be cloudy.

Cocktails should be served and drunk without delay, otherwise they lose their freshness and flavour.

The most famous cocktail is the martini. The original recipe consisted of equal parts of gin and sweet or dry vermouth, according to taste. Changing tastes have made a drier mixture more popular. A word of warning is indicated regarding martinis. In some establishments it has become the practice when a martini is ordered to serve a straight vermouth with a slice of lemon and a dash of lemonade, therefore one has to state quite clearly what is required when ordering a martini.

Some popular cocktails

Dry martini

$\frac{2}{3}$ Dry gin
$\frac{1}{3}$ Dry vermouth
  Zest of lemon
  Serve with an olive on a cocktail stick
  Prepare in a mixing glass
  Stir and strain

Sweet martini

$\frac{2}{3}$ Dry gin
$\frac{1}{3}$ Sweet vermouth
  Serve with a cherry on a cocktail stick
  Prepare in a mixing glass
  Stir and strain

113

Manhattan
$\frac{2}{3}$ Rye whiskey
$\frac{1}{3}$ Sweet vermouth
Dash of angostura bitters
serve with a cherry on a cocktail stick
prepare in a mixing glass
stir and strain

Alexander
$\frac{1}{2}$ Brandy
$\frac{1}{4}$ Crême de cacao
$\frac{1}{4}$ Fresh cream
Shake in cocktail shaker

White Lady
$\frac{1}{2}$ Dry gin
$\frac{1}{4}$ Cointreau
$\frac{1}{4}$ Lemon juice
Shake in cocktail shaker

Bronx
$\frac{1}{2}$ Dry gin
$\frac{1}{6}$ Dry vermouth
$\frac{1}{6}$ Sweet vermouth
$\frac{1}{6}$ Fresh orange juice
Shake in cocktail shaker

Collins
Tall glass
2 oz (6 cl) Dry gin
2 oz (6 cl) lemon juice
1 tspoon caster sugar
Shake and strain
Fill up with soda
Dash of angostura bitters
Serve with straws

Champagne Cocktail
1 Lump of sugar soaked in angostura bitters
1 Slice of fresh orange
Top glass up with champagne
Dash of brandy is optional

Whisky sour

1 oz (3 cl) lemon juice
$\frac{1}{2}$ teaspoon caster sugar
2 oz (6 cl) Whisky (usually Bourbon whiskey)
Shake in cocktail shaker and strain
Fill up with soda
Add a slice of lemon
A few drops of egg white will improve the froth on the drink this
'sour' can also be made with brandy, gin or rum.

Note
That it is not safe to shake a mineral or effervescent drink in a cocktail
shaker.

The classically accepted partnerships of food and wine

There are no hard and fast rules about wine and food. The choice is a very
personal one. Helpful guidelines however, are: light wines before fuller
ones, dry before sweet, red before sweet white, lesser wines before fine
wines.

When one wine only is served throughout a meal it should be the wine
most appropriate to the main course.

Champagne is regarded as a suitable wine to be served throughout a meal.

Some foods do not take kindly to wine, such as highly spiced foods,
like curries. These are better partnered with water or lager. Vinegar is an
enemy of wine as are citrus fruits and chocolate.

Type of food/course	Suitable wine types
Aperitif	Dry sherry, cocktails
Hors d'oeuvres	Dry sherry
Soup	Medium dry sherry
Fish	Dry white wine, hock or mosel
Entrées	Light claret or fine light white wine
White meat/poultry	Bordeaux, Burgundy, Côtes du Rhone
Red meats/roasts/game	A strong red wine of aromatic savour, fine vintage Bordeaux or Burgundy
Cold buffet	Medium dry rosé wines
Sweets	Champagne, natural sweet wines
Cheese	Tawny port
Fruit	Champagne, sauternes, mellow wines
Coffee	Cognac, liqueurs

QUESTIONS

1 What is the correct way to handle a glass?
2 What steps should be followed when cleaning glasses?
3 At what temperature should red wines be served?
4 How should a bottle of champagne be opened?
5 What are the guidelines for choosing wine to match foods?

ACTIVITIES

1 Prepare a list of popular drinks served with meals and describe a suitable glass for each drink.
2 Select a number of different sized bottles and calculate the outage from each one, using different types of glass.

Part II — Wines, Spirits and Liqueurs

The wines of many countries have become known and popular since people started travelling abroad on holiday and on business. Sampling the wine of the country, acquiring a taste for a particular wine, and asking for these wines when they return home, resulting in a substantial increase in wine sales in Britain with a wider selection.

The Wines of France
The greatest of the wine growing countries, with centuries of tradition and expertise, France has a large and varied choice of wines to suit all tastes.

Champagne
The most famous of all the sparkling wines is grown and bottled in the carefully defined area known as Champagne, which comprises the principal regions of Montagne de Reims, Marne Valley and Epernay, and Côtes des Blancs.

The main varieties of grapes used are the Pinot Noir and the White Chardonnay; grapes of great delicacy. Production is limited strictly to these districts and french law refuses to allow districts outside this region to classify their wines as Champagne. The labels and corks must bear the appellation Champagne and when appropriate, the vintage year.

In late autumn the grapes are gathered and pressed and the juice pumped into casks. The first fermentation transforms the juice into wine and after several months when the wine has reached the necessary degree of clarity, the blend or cuvée is made up by experienced tasters.

The art of blending in vats of different vintages or different vineyards ensures a unique individual character.

The secondary fermentation in bottles under pressure produces the sparkle and effervescence. This secondary fermentation was discovered and controlled by Dom Perignon, a Benedictine monk, who was in charge of the cellars at the Abbey of Hautvilliers in the seventeenth century. The quantity of sugar and old wine added determines whether the champagne will be dry, extra dry, medium or sweet.

Brut is a very dry champagne made without any sugar at all. Champagne should be served very cool, but not iced.

Champagne is bottled in various sizes: quarter, half and full size bottles; magnums (two bottles); jeroboams (four bottles); rehoboams (six bottles); methuselahs (eight bottles); and nebuchadnezzar (twenty bottles).

The interests of the champagne industry are looked after in France by a special committee, the CIVC (Comité Interprofessionel du Vin de Champagne)

Some principal brands are: *Bollinger; Veuve Cliquot; Moet et Chandon; Heidsieck Dry Monopole; Krug; G. H. Mumm (Cordon Rouge and Cordon Vert); Piper Heidsieck; Pol Roger; Pommery; Louis Roederer.*

Bordeaux

Bordeaux lies at the heart of the great vineyards which produce the finest and noblest wines of France. Both red and white wines are produced in the region with the red wine predominating. The fine red wines, known as Clarets, are noted for their delicate bouquet, brilliant colour, subtle flavour and fullness without heaviness. From the Sauternes district south of the city come the great sweet white wines.

So numerous and varied are the wines and vineyards of Bordeaux that they rival each other in their excellence and elegance. Each has its own individual character.

The Cabernet-Sauvignon, Cabernet Franc and Merlot are the important red wine grapes; Sauvignon Blanc and Semillon for the white.

The Médoc area produces the magnificient château bottled clarets in the principal communes of: Pauillac; Margaux; St Estèphe; and St Julien. The other main regions of Bordeaux are: St Emillion; Pomerol, Graves and Sauternes.

The district to the south of Médoc known as Graves, produces a large quantity of excellent white wine. Its great reds are equivalent to some of the Medocs.

Château haut brion is the most famous of the Graves clarets.

The Sauternes and Barsac districts are the home of the world famous rich white wines. The most eminent of these is *Château d'Yquem*. For the best wines, the white grapes of Sauternes are not considered sufficiently ripe until they appear wrinkled and over-ripe and have been affected by 'noble rot' or 'pourriture noble', which is an over-ripening of the grape before picking. The result is a very sweet golden wine, a natural dessert wine.

Burgundy

The vineyards of Burgundy cover a vast area, the most famous department, the Côte d'Or, producing the finest red burgundies which have been renowned for centuries.

The Côte d'Or comprises two of the most famous important productive areas, the Côte de Nuits and the Côte de Beaune. From the Côte de Nuits come the finest red wines of Burgundy, rich, glowing and full-bodied, with appreciable bouquet. The most celebrated of them are *Nuits St Georges* and *Chambertin.* The Pinot Noir is the grape used in the great burgundies.

The Côte de Beaune produces red and white wines of distinction, smooth velvety reds, which however, fall short of the best of the reds from the Côte de Nuits. The white wines are outstanding for their charm, and elegant bouquet. Among the notable reds are *Beaune, Corton* and *Pommard.* The finest white burgundies of the Côte d'Or are produced from the communes of Puligny-Montrachet and Chassagne Montrachet, superlative wines of rare quality with a beautiful bouquet. From the Communes of Meursault come white wines with wonderful delicacy and fresh fruity aroma. The best of the white burgundies is produced in the Côte de Beaune exclusively from the Chardonnay grape.

A natural continuation of the Côte de Beaune is Chalonnaise. Here is produced red, white and sparkling wines, the reds, full and fragrant, are good standard wines.

Further south, Maconnais on the Beaujolais border is principally renowned for the pale delicate dry wine, *Pouilly-Fuissé.*

In Beaujolais, the Gamay grape imparts the quality and refreshing fruitiness which distinguishes the extremely pleasant and satisfying Beaujolais wines, *Brouilly, Juliénas,* etc.

Chablis in the extreme north of Burgundy produces possibly the most bone dry wine in the world, noted for its distinctive flavour and colour. It is very pale with greenish glints, made from the Chardonnay grape. The Premier Growths include, Les Preuses and Grenouilles. *Chablis* is one of the world's classic wines.

Côtes-du-Rhône

On both sides of the river Rhône in the area between Lyon and Avignon, lie the vineyards of the Côtes-du-Rhône. In this region there are great variations in climatic conditions and types of vines which are reflected in the white, red and rosé wines.

The white wines of the Côte Rotie in the north, have an individual character and dryness; the principal appellations are *Château Grillet* and *Condrieu.*

Some of the white wines from the south can be notable, especially from the light sandy soils of Laudun and Lirac. *Tavel,* the most famous of the Rhône rosé wines, comes from the most southerly end of the Rhône valley. This fresh light fruity wine is particularly pleasing in its gleaming pink colour. The fine red wines of the north, rich in bouquet and deep in colour, include the red *Hermitage,* dark, yet delicate and mellow; and *Cornas,* deep red and elegant.

The southern Côtes-du-Rhône reds are notable for lightness and delicacy. Most notable names are *Gigondas* and *Cairanne.* The noble *Châteauneuf-du-Pape* is one of the world's distinguished classical wines, deep red and robust with a powerful bouquet, soft and fruit scented.

A very small quantity of white Châteauneuf-du-Pape is still produced in this area.

Provence, Languedoc and Roussillon

Provence, Languedoc and Roussillon play a major part in the output of the French VDQS (Vins Délimités de Qualité Supérieure) wines. This is the area of the everyday wine, simple and refreshing. In Provence there are a few AC (Appellation Contrôllée) wines. The best of them are *Cassis, Palette* and *Bandol.*

In Languedoc and Roussillon some of the wines which have established a reputation are the AC Blanquette de Limoux, a sparkling white, pale, dry and refreshing wine, and the red Fitou dessert wines of the region. Those from the area near Perpignan are better known for their sweet aromatic flavour, the best of AC being *Banyuls* and *Rivesaltes.*

Loire

The river Loire links the wine growing areas from Auvergne to Brittany, incorporating Orleans, Touraine and Anjou.

The white sweet wines of Anjou are smooth and fruit scented, especially noteworthy, AC wines are *Bonnezeaux* and *Quart de Chaume*. The light red flower scented wines of Touraine such as *Chinon* and *Bourgueil* are the classic red wines of the Loire made from the Cabernet-Franc grape.

The well known pinks of the Loire, the *Rosé d'Anjou* are young fresh wines. The best of these, the *Anjou Rosé de Cabernet*, is made only with the Cabernet-Franc grape.

The best of the sparkling and semi-sparkling wines of Vouvray and Saumur are made according to the 'Méthode Champenoise', the dry (still or sparkling), have a hint of background sweetness. *Vouvray* is an Appellation Contrôllée, as is *Montlouis*.

Among the best known wines of the upper Loire are *Sancerre* and *Pouilley Fumé*. The Sauvignon blanc grape or blanc fumé is the only grape used. It imparts the crisp, fruity yet dry flavour and smokey aroma for which these wines are notable.

Muscadet is a very dry crisp white wine from the country around Nantes near the mouth of the Loire. It shares its name with the Muscadet grape from which it is produced.

Sèvre-et-Maine is reputedly the best of the muscadets.

Alsace

On the eastern slopes of the Vosges, the vineyards of Alsace lie along the French side of the Rhine.

The wines are named after the grapes from which they are produced, notably the white Riesling, Sylvaner and Gewurztraminer; and are bottled in distinctive tall slender green bottles. It is the rule that only wines bottled in Alsace are entitled to the Appellation Contrôllée, 'Alsace'.

'Alsace Grand Cru', is an appellation which is more definitive, and recognises the best wines from designated vineyards long regarded as exceptional. They must be made solely from the 'Noble' grapes, Riesling, Gewurztraminer, Pinot Gris or Muscat.

The wines of Germany

German wines fall into the following main categories: *Deutscher Tafelwein*, German table wine which is a hundred per cent ordinary German wine or Tafelwein, which can be German wine blended with a percentage of other wine from another district or EEC country, from approved regions.

Qualitätswein Bestimmter Anbaugebiete (QBA); quality wine from a defined district that must not be blended with wines from any other area of production. These wines are subject to certain testing requirements and are controlled by a numbered label.

Qualitätswein mit Pradikat (QMP) is the top quality wine, strictly controlled by tasting and testing. No added sweetening is allowed and the wine has to be produced exclusively from a single district within a defined growing region. The wine can be identified by that district.

There are innumerable classifications given to German wines and these give a clear indication of the wine type. *Kabinett* is the basic QMP. *Spätlese* indicates the late gathering of ripe grapes and consequently the wine is sweeter and fuller bodied.

Auslese wines are made from the finest ripest grapes, specially selected to make fine sweet wines. *Beerenauslese*; over-ripe berries, are individually selected; *Trockenbeerenauslese*, indicates that the grapes have been left until shrivelled and the action of, 'Noble Rot', or Edelfaule gives them intensity of flavour and sweetness.

One of the rarest German wines is *Eiswein*, which is only produced when climatic conditions are right and a particularly early frost coincides with a late harvest. The grapes become frozen on the vine overnight and are picked in that state to produce a delicate sweet and unusual wine. Eiswein must be followed by a description of Kabinett, Spätlese, etc.

The finest wines of the river Rhine and Mosel are made from the classic Riesling grape. Other wines come from grape varieties such as Sylvaner, Traminer and Muller-Thurgau. Sometimes stated on the label.

The main wine regions in Germany are the Rhine districts of Rheingau, Rheinhessen and Rheinpfalz, The Nahe, Franconia and The Mosel.

German wines are bottled in green bottles for Mosel, Saar and Ruwer, and in brown bottles for Rhine and Nahe wines. The terms Hock and Moselle are sometimes used to describe the style of glasses used for these wines.

The Rheingau district predominates in wines of maturity and character from the large estates of Schloss Vollrads and Schloss Johannisberg. The Rheinhessen produces soft and sweetish wines from the Sylvaner and Muller-Thurgau grapes. Best known of these wines are *Liebfraumilch* and *Niersteiner*.

Germany's largest vineyard producing wine from a variety of grapes is the Rheinpfalz or Palatinate. Here wines are full and soft. The wine commune is 'Bad Durkheim'.

The Nahe produces some of the finest white wines, combining the excellent qualities of the Rhine and Mosel, fresh flowery and fruity. Bad Kreuznach is the main wine centre where some of the best vineyards are located. In the upper regions of the Nahe is Schloss Bockelheim, where the famous vineyard of Schlossbockelheimer Kupfergrübe is situated.

The middle mosel wines of classic quality from the Riesling grape are distinctive in fragrance and charm. The famous *Piesporter Goldtröpfchen* and *Bernkasteler Dokter* originate from this area. From the Saar and Ruwer tributaries in a particularly good year the wine can surpass the best of German wine for elegance and breed. Franconia is an area on the river Main which has a long history in wine dating back to the Roman era. The name *Steinwein* is used generally for Franconian wines, best recognised for the flagon shaped bottles or green Bocksbeutel. The bottle design is protected by German law for Franconia. The Sylvaner grape is used almost exclusively and the white wines are fairly dry. Few are exported.

The wines of Italy

Italy is one of the largest wine producing countries of the world. There are very few areas where wine is not produced and the variation in climate from the cold Alps in the north to the almost tropical heat of Sicily in the south, produces a wide variety of wine for every taste.

The Italian Government has laid down standards of control for wine, similar in part to the French Appellation Controlee, which has improved the quality of Italian wine.

The Denominazione di Origine Controllata (DOC) is a guarantee that the wine has reached a standard of quality, is produced from an agreed area, is properly aged, contains specific grapes and complies with traditonal methods of production. Such a wine must carry the DOC. label on the bottle.

The top rank Denominazione di Origine Controllata Garantita, (DOCG) is a standard awarded only to top quality wines which comply with very stringent regulations. A formal application must be made to the Ministry of Agriculture and a complete investigation is carried out by an inspector. The vintner takes upon himself the responsibility of adhering to the strict regulations, one of which is that the wine must be bottled and sealed with a special government seal.

Most of the major regions have been declared DOC and this has inspired confidence in the quality, resulting in an increase in exported wines.

Italy has always been renowned for the fine red wines produced in Piemonte, Tuscany and Verona. The two finest of these from Piemonte in the north are *Barola* and *Barberesco*, which take their names from the villages. Both are full in flavour and scent with Barberesco lighter and slightly drier. The Nebbiolo grape is used.

From Asti come still and sparkling wines. The best known fragrant *Asti Spumante* is produced from the Moscato grape of Asti. Other excellent wines of Piemonte take the name of their grapes. *Nebbiolo, Grignolino* and *Barbera.*

The Veneto or Verona region produces excellent wine of quality. *Valpolicella*, one of the most popular red wines, is bright cherry red with a soft light flavour. *Bardolino* is fresh clear red, and *Soave*, perhaps Italy's most highly regarded white wine, should be drunk young and very cool.

Tuscany is the home of *Chianti*, often recognised by the straw covered flasks, although the best Chianti is distinguished by its claret shaped bottles.

The name Chianti is restricted and Chianti Classico reserved for wine from the central and best district. It is aged in oak for a period of three to five years (riserva). The insignia on the neck of the bottle for Chianti Classico is a black cockerel. A cherub identifies the other Chianti vineyards.

The wines of America

America produces a wide range of wines of all types. Californian wines, particularly from the Napa Valley district, can be compared favourably with any of the fine classic wines.

There is a strong resemblance between Californian and European wines.

Many of the grape varieties in use were originally transplanted from their homeland and flourished extremely well in the mild climate and long dry growing season of California.

The label names of some of the premier wines are identified with the variety of classic grape used. The *Cabernet Sauvignons; Chardonnays* and *Pinot Noir* wines are among the finest examples.

The quality of varietally named wines depends largely upon the amount of grape variety contained in the wine. Regulations require a minimum of fifty one per cent of the grape named on the label, but the remainder may be made up of any ordinary less expensive grape. Proposed amendments to increase this minimum percentage will result in an improvement in the standards and quality of the average varietally named wines. Wine production has expanded due to increased demand at home and abroad, and advances in wine research and technology are providing excellent young fresh tasting wines in a matter of weeks.

American wine history encompasses some four hundred years, but the advent of prohibition destroyed an industry which is now, through revolutionary changes in wine growing and wine drinking, presenting a serious challenge to the established wine producers of the old world.

English wines

The areas of viticulture in Britain lie mainly in the southern regions of England.

Centuries ago monks were responsible for the cultivation of the vineyards belonging to the monasteries, but various setbacks from bad summers, the effects of the plague and the dissolution of the monasteries, decimated and ultimately destroyed a once thriving industry. Interest is once again being shown in English wines grown and bottled in English vineyards, many of them on, or close to the original mediaeval vineyards.

One of these sites, which was established by the Abbots of Glastonbury in the twelth century, is Pilton Manor vineyard at Pilton in Somerset, where vines have been replanted and are producing white wines of quality.

Fortified wines

Fortified wines are so called because the natural alcohol content has been increased by the addition of spirit, usually grape brandy. The principal fortified wines are sherry, port, Madeira and marsala. Legislation protects these wines in Europe.

Spanish sherry comes from Jerez and the defined area of Jerez de la Frontera in Southern Spain.

Port comes only from Portugal and only from the area of the upper Douro Valley in Northern Portugal where the area is delimited.

Madeira is from the Island of Madeira.

Marsala is a famous sweet wine and principal Italian dessert wine produced in Sicily.

Fortified wines are not generally drunk with a meal and feature more as pre-meal or after-meal drinks.

Spirits

Whisky
Whisky is a grain spirit obtained by distilling a mash of malted and fermented barley, rye and maize, and is the world's best known spirit.

Bourbon whiskey is distilled in the USA from a fermented mash of grain, not less than half is maize. It takes its name from Bourbon county in Kentucky, where it was first made. *Rye*, or *Canadian whisky* is a straight whisky distilled from a fermented mash of grain, not less than half of which is rye. *Irish whiskey* is a grain spirit distilled in pot stills from malted barley, and differs from Scotch whisky in flavour due to the different methods of production.

Scotch whisky
Whisky, or 'Usquebaugh' (water of life), originated in Ireland and in the fifteenth century the art of distilling whisky found its way to Scotland via the Western Isles. Its popularity soon spread over the mainland and into the Highlands, where stills were operated by individuals for their own needs.

The taste for whisky spread further afield, to the Lowlands and to England and with the growing demand came the need for control and the recognition of a source of considerable revenue.

Today whisky is one of the largest exports from the United Kingdom. In the production of Scotch whisky there are three essentials: the barley, the yeast and good soft water. Mountain or natural spring water is preferred.

The 'Highland Line' is an imaginary line drawn across Scotland from Dundee in the east of Greenock in the west and traditionally divides the country into the Highlands and the Lowlands. Scotch whisky is only genuine Scotch if it is made from a spirit obtained by distillation in Scotland, from a cereal grain mash, sugared by the diastase of malt, fermented by the action of the yeast and matured in cask for a minimum period of three years.

The main types of single malt whisky are: *Campbeltown malts* from The Mull of Kintyre, *Islay malts* from the Island of Islay, *Highland malts* from the biggest area of production around (Inverness and Aberdeen and *Lowland malts* from around Glasgow and Edinburgh. The area of Speyside in the Highlands has the biggest concentration of distilleries and is generally considered to be the source of the finest malt whiskies. Malt whisky is made exclusively from malted barley and is double distilled in large heated copper pot stills.

The first distillation produces a coarse weak liquid known as 'low wines', which is passed through for a second distillation to remove impurities and increase the alcoholic strength. After the distillation process is completed the spirit is pumped into vats prior to filling into oak casks, which often have been sherry casks and impart a subtle flavour and slight colour to the spirit. The casks are then stored in dark airy warehouses to mature quietly and slowly. When the casks emerge they contain fine mellow malt whisky and the three years minimum maturing period is considered young whisky whereas a period of between eight and twelve years produces a more perfect malt.

The most popular and best selling Scotch whisky is undoubtedly grain or blended whisky, distilled from a mash of malt barley and unmalted cereals, mostly maize. The process of distillation takes place in a continuous still, patented by an Irishman named Aeneas Coffey in 1831. This is a faster method than the pot still and is cheaper to operate. A percentage of malted barley must always be added to the mashing process to provide the diastase needed to convert the starch of the unmalted grain to maltose. The grain or blended whiskies are distilled mainly in the Glasgow and Edinburgh areas south of the 'Highland Line'.

The art and objective of blending is to combine the characteristics of various whiskies to provide a blend to a particular formula. Whisky is colourless when first distilled but a limited amount of colouring by caramel is permitted.

Although Scotch whisky can often be used as a base for mixed drinks, its full flavour is best appreciated if taken either neat or with water.

Brandy or Cognac

Brandy is a spirit which is produced from the fermented juice of fresh grapes and can be made in any wine growing country. The finest brandy comes from the Cognac region in the area between the river Charente and north of the Gironde estuary in the west coast of France.

Only brandy produced in this area is entitled to bear the Appellation Controleé 'Cognac'.

Cognac is distilled from the pot still method and two distillations are necessary to produce the clear white spirit which is run into casks of Limousin oak to mature for a legal minimum period of two years.

These casks play an important part in the mellowing process of the spirit imparting a special flavour, and pale golden tint, particularly to the VSOP (Very Special Old Pale) Cognacs which spend five years or more maturing in such casks. The main classifications of area are:

1 Grande Champagne
2 Petite Champagne
3 Borderies
4 Fins Bois
5 Bons Bois
6 Bois Ordinaire
7 Bois Communs

Armagnac

Armagnac from Gascony in western France is the oldest of the brandies, less famous than Cognac, but more robust. It ages in casks of black oak which impart flavour and colour. Bas-Armagnac or Black Armagnac, is particularly sought after, and the best compares favourably in quality to Cognac.

As with Cognac the maturing and marketing of Armagnac are controlled by strict regulations.

Rum

Rum is a spirit distilled from fermented cane sugar or molasses, which is the dark residue of the cane juice which has been boiled to first extract the sugar. The stalks of the sugar cane are crushed in roller mills and the juice is collected and purified by heating. The water in the juice evaporates, to leave behind a syrup which with low heating gradually crystallises. This granulated syrup is then transferred to large centrifugal drums which revolve rapidly, extracting the sugar crystals and leaving behind thick treacly molasses. A second boiling of the molasses produces sugar of a lower grade, and the resulting molasses is now ready to be transferred to a rum distillery where it is mixed with water and fermenting agents, which can vary according to the area. In Jamaica, for example, the residue from previous distillations, known as dunder, is stored and fermented, and used to start off the fermentation in a continuous and hereditary process. When this wash, as it is known, is fermented out, it is distilled to produce rum.

Rum differs according to various factors: the yeasts used, the variety of cane, the soil and the method of distillation, either pot or continuous still. When it leaves the still it is colourless, and the colour is imparted by the addition of burnt sugar or caramel according to type. Rum is stored in casks to mature and must legally be three years old before being sold in Britain. The different types of Rum are:

Jamaica rum very popular in Britain, soft flavoured, pungent, delicate, golden brown.

Demerara rum from Guyana, very dark coloured, rich full flavoured rum, less pungent than Jamaica rum.

Bacardi rum white rum, formerly from Cuba, now from various sources including Barbados, Nassau or Puerto Rico where the classical Carta Blanca Bacardi rum is produced.

Gin

Gin is considered to be the purest of all spirits and is distilled from grain, usually maize, flavoured mainly with juniper berries. The French for juniper is Genievre or Geneva, and this eventually became shortened to gin. The first two stages of distillation are in a patent still, and the third in a pot still, where the various constituents are added for flavouring and include juniper berries, coriander seeds, angelica, orris roots and orange peel.

Gin is a versatile spirit and can be mixed with juices and used as a base for cocktails. It is ready to drink within a few days of manufacture.

Vodka

Vodka is a pure spirit which at one time was produced from a variety of materials but today is distilled mainly from rye. In Russian, Vodka means 'little water' and as early as the twelfth century it was used solely for medicinal purposes.

By the fourteenth century it was being distilled in other countries and as it became more popular its use spread to Europe. At the beginning vodka contained unpleasant oils which spoilt the taste, and to offset this, various herbs, berries and fruits were infused into it. Russian vodka retains these characteristics and should be drunk neat and cold. Other vodkas, including British types, which are unflavoured, are eminently suitable for cocktails and mixed drinks.

Today the pure grain spirit is scientifically and lengthily filtered through charcoal to a high degree of purification, and left unflavoured for a dry unsweetened vodka. Sweetening and flavouring may be added according to the formula of a particular blend.

Liqueurs

A liqueur, an after dinner drink, is a perfect finish to a meal as it is said to have a beneficial effect on the digestive system. This is hardly surprising in view of the fact that the monastic orders are accreditied with the original formulas.

The infusion of distilled spirits with sundry herbs, spices and fruits resulted in mellow liqueurs of a high alcoholic content, which were used essentially for medicinal purposes.

The monks kept their highly prized formulas a secret, and the recipes were handed down from generation to generation. The most famous of these are Benedictine and Chartreuse.

Advocaat   Dutch brandy with egg yolks, low alcoholic content

Angelica   A very sweet yellow liqueur flavoured with angelica, basque country.

Anisette   French; aniseed flavour; very sweet

Apricot Brandy   Highly flavoured; distilled from fresh apricots and their kernels.

Aurum   Italian; pale gold; highly aromatic; orange flavour.

Benedictine   Oldest; fecamp in 1510 by Benedictine monks; very sweet and aromatic; distinctive bottle with DOM label (Deo Optimo Maximo).

Creme de Cacao   Very sweet chocolate flavour; Chauao in Venezuela for best cocoa beans.

Chartreuse   High alchoholic strength if green; yellow is not so potent and much sweeter; made by Carthusian monks from secret formula, the genuine liqueur has lith.alier on the left hand corner of the label. This liqueur is highly aromatic.

Cherry Brandy   Juice from ripe cherries and crushed cherry stones.

Cointreau   French colourless orange curacao in distinctive square bottle; triple sec.

Creme de Menthe   Wine or grain spirit flavoured with peppermint; digestive properties.

Curacao   Wine or grain spirit with bitter oranges from Dutch West Indies.

127

Spirit

Add hot coffee

Pour in cream

Float cream on top of coffee

Drambuie   Scotch whisky and honey base, world famours; made in Scotland.

Goldwasser (Danzig)   Colourless with an aniseed and orange flavour with flakes of gold.

Galliano   Italian liqueur; intriguing flavour.

Grand Marnier   French brandy liqueur; orange flavour; golden brown.

Kahlua   Mexican coffee liqueur.

Kummel   Distilled from grain; caraway seed and cumin flavour; digestive.

Kirsch   White brandy distilled from whole cherries with their stones.

Maraschino   Cherry flavoured liqueur; Italian.

Mirabelle   French plum flavoured liqueur; colourless.

Sambuca   Italian aniseed liqueur.

Strega   Italian; light colour; not very sweet.

Tia Maria   Jamaican rum flavoured with coffee.

Tangao   Tangerine flavoured brandy liqueur.

Van der Hum   Tangerine flavoured liqueur from South Africa.

Speciality coffees

As a speciality, various spirits and liqueurs can, when combined with hot coffee and fresh double cream floated on top, be served in a goblet glass, and presented attractively on a small doily covered plate. The sugar if required should be put into the glass first, then the measure of the appropriate spirit or liqueur added. Place a teaspoon in the glass to act as a conductor and prevent the glass from cracking. Pour in the coffee and stir to dissolve the sugar and mix in the spirit. The addition of sugar helps the cream to float. The cream should be poured slowly over the back or into the bowl of a teaspoon held over the surface of the coffee or it can be poured slowly down the side of the glass. An even layer of cream should float on top of the hot liquid without mixing into it.

This speciality should be done at a side table in front of the customer so that they can appreciate the skills in the process. Techniques such as this are a great aid to sales promotion. Some suggested speciality coffees can be prepared from the following liquors:

Speciality coffee	Liquor base	
Gaelic coffee	Scotch Whisky	
Irish coffee	Irish Whiskey	
Dutch coffee	Hollands' Gin	
Russian coffee	Vodka	Hot black coffee is added in each case and fresh double cream floated on top of the drink.
Caribbean coffee	Rum	
Normandy coffee	Calvados	
German coffee	Kirsch	
Calypso coffee	Tia Maria	
Coffee Royale (French)	Cognac	
Witch's coffee	Strega	
Aquavit coffee	Aquavit	
Mexican coffee	Kahlua	

QUESTIONS

1 Name the five main wine districts of France.
2 What is distinctive about German wine bottles?
3 What is a fortified wine?
4 Describe the making of Cognac
5 Name and describe five different liqueurs.

ACTIVITIES

1 Prepare a list of the different brands of Scotch Whisky.
2 On a map of Central Europe, identify the different districts that you
   have read about, where wine is produced.

Part III — Soft Drinks, Tea and Coffee

Soft drinks
There are various soft drinks which come under the following headings:

Natural mineral waters
Aerated mineral waters
Fruit squashes
Fruit juices
Syrups

Natural mineral waters
These are well known for their health giving and curative properties. They originate from natural springs in the ground becoming impregnated with mineral salts in the process. Some also have natural aeration. They can be found in different countries and are identified by their place of origin. ie Vichy, Vittel, Evian. They are best drunk well-chilled.

Other mineral waters such as Perrier, Malvern, Apollinaris, etc, are suitable for inclusion in drinks and are often used in place of soda water or plain water.

Aerated mineral waters (artificial)
Mineral waters such as lemonade, ginger beer, ginger ale and tonic water are made from a syrup of sugar and water which is filtered, coloured and flavoured with various essences, purified water with carbon dioxide is added.

Fruit squashes
These are made from the juices of fresh fruit with preservative and are concentrated.

Fruit juices
These are made from the juices of fresh fruit with preservative and sweetening added, filtered to prevent fermentation.

Syrups
These are made from a sugar and water syrup with colouring and flavouring added. They require dilution and are used as a constituent in cocktails. The following flavours are available:
Gomme (pure sugar, clear); cerise (cherry); cassis (blackcurrant); orange; citron (lemon); fraise (strawberry); framboise (raspberry); grenadine (pomegranate); groseille (gooseberry); menthe (mint); banane (banana); orgeat (almond).

Tea
Tea can be served at various times of the day, early morning, breakfast, afternoon, or at night, depending on the facilities provided. The still-room is normally responsibile for preparing the tea for the service personnel.

Tea bags are in general use, but where loose tea is being used a measured dispenser is essential as strict portion control is necessary.

The equipment used, teapot, hot water jug, sugar bowl and milk jug, must be checked for cleanliness, and the teapot heated. A measured amount of tea or teabags should be placed in the teapot and fresh boiling water poured into the teapot and allowed to infuse for a few minutes.

Tea is not generally poured for the guests, but served by placing the teapot and hot water jug on the table to the right for guests to serve themselves.

There are a number of varieties of tea that are commonly served:

China tea
Pale and delicate in flavour, this tea should be served in a china teapot. No milk is offered, only sugar and slices of lemon.

Russian tea
Normally freshly brewed Indian or Ceylon tea is used. The tea is served in a glass contained in a silver holder with a handle. This is presented on a small doily covered plate. A slice of lemon is placed in the tea. Sugar is offered, but not milk.

Iced tea
Strong freshly brewed tea, chilled and served in a tall glass, presented on a doily covered small plate, with a slice of lemon in the glass or served separately. Ice can be added if desired.

Coffee

Coffee is the most common non-alcoholic beverage served as part of a meal. It is normally served during breakfast as an alternative to tea; as a mid-morning drink; after luncheon or dinner; and sometimes as a late night beverage. Although coffee drinking originated in the middle east and did not spread to Europe until the seventeenth century, it is now truly an international drink in the modern world.

Coffee is an infusion made from the roasted seed of the coffee bush berry, grown in hot climates of the Middle East, India, Java, Kenya and Brazil. It has little or no nutritional value but is said to be a good stimulant due to the caffein content.

Preparation of coffee
There are a number of methods of preparing coffee. The main principle is to extract the aroma and flavour of the coffee bean without causing bitterness. Boiling water or steam is passed through the ground coffee and strained or filtered into a serving vessel.

Jug method or cafetiere
The simplest method is where freshly ground coffee is placed into a warmed jug and boiling water added. After a short period of infusion the grounds are caused to sink to the bottom and the liquid coffee may be poured off. In a plain jug a spoon drawn across the surface grounds will cause them to sink. In a cafetiere there is a fine gauze plunger for this operation.

Vacuum infusion or 'cona'

For many years the most popular method was vacuum infusion, a method popularly referred to as cona coffee. In this preparation, water is boiled in a glass flask and allowed to expand and rise up a glass tube into a second open container which is fitted tightly on top of the water flask. A glass draining rod sits in the top of the tube and the coffee grains are placed in this upper container.

As the water boils and rises into the top container it infuses with the coffee grains. The heat is removed and the resultant vacuum in the lower flask draws the liquid coffee down whilst the glass draining rod holds back the spent grains. This method was often carried out in front of the guest and created great interest in the process.

Still and espresso

Where large quantities of coffee are required or there is a constant demand, special water and steam boilers are used. Most large restaurants and hotels have a hot water boiler and coffee maker called a still. The operation is straightforward.

A measured amount of ground coffee is placed in an infusion jug which is then fitted into the machine so that boiling water can be sprayed through the grains and along a series of tubes into a storage urn, where the temperature can be maintained. The infusion jug contains a filter which prevents the grains from being carried into the finished brew.

If demand is fluctuating and it is not viable to prepare large quantities of coffee in anticipation, an expresso machine can be used. Steam is passed at high pressure through small quantities of very finely ground coffee and one or two cups of concentrated coffee can be made at a time very quickly. This method is ideal for cafes and coffee shops.

Filter coffee (or pour and serve)

Perhaps the most convenient and simplest method of all is the filter method. Originally this was done in a specially designed earthenware French coffee pot with an infusion jar fitted on top, but recent developments have produced a highly efficient filter machine which has its own reservoir and high speed water heater.

A measured quantity of finely ground coffee is placed in a special filter paper fitted into the machine. Cold water is poured into the reservoir and almost instantly a flow of boiled water is fed down onto the grains and filters through into the jug on a hotplate.

Other methods

For domestic use, a small version of the pour and serve or filter machine is available. Electric and gas coffee percolators are also popular. The basic principle of coffee making however remains the same. Boiling water or steam must be fresh and the quantity and grind size carefully monitored. Never prepare coffee far in advance as it will lose aroma and flavour when stored for too long. Under no circumstances should it be allowed to boil as this will impart a bitterness.

Instant coffee

A commercially produced soluble coffee powder was developed at the beginning of the twentieth century and is now available in a number of forms. This product should not be confused with fresh bean coffee, as it only requires to be dissolved in hot water or milk.

Coffee service

Tastes in coffee vary considerably and the variety of blends available is immense. Strong highly roasted beans are preferred for French breakfast coffee and Italian espresso, whilst more delicate flavours like Mocha or Kenya are popular for everyday drinking. Richer blends, sometimes with additives of fig or chicory are often taken after dinner and a variety of speciality coffees can be made with liqueurs and spirits. Coffee can be served on its own or with cream or hot milk.

A de-caffinated coffee is available for those who do not like the stimulating effect and instant coffee or coffee bags can be used for convenience.

QUESTIONS

1 Name five different types of soft drink.
2 Name and describe five soft drinks that are used as constituents in cocktails.
3 What is the correct procedure for serving tea?
4 Give a detailed definition of coffee.
5 Explain three different methods of preparing fresh coffee.

ACTIVITIES

1 Prepare a list of the different varieties of soft drink that would require to be stocked for the smooth running of a cocktail bar.
2 Calculate the cheapest method of preparing a cup of coffee.

Glossary of Menu Terms

À la	In the style
À la Carte	Individually chosen and priced
À la King	Diced meat in a cream sauce
Amandine	With almond
Aperitif	Pre-meal drink
Aspic	Meat jelly
Au gratin	Sprinkled with crumbs or cheese and browned
Baba	Sponge
Ballotine	Stuffed meat roll
Bavarois	Light whipped jelly cream
Bearnaise	Rich butter sauce with tarragon
Beignet	Fritter
Bisque	Rich cream shellfish soup
Blanquette	White stew with onion and lamb or veal
Bleu	Boiled alive (fish): very rare (steak)
Bombay Duck	Dried Indian fish
Bombe	Moulded ice cream
Bordelaise	In rich brown sauce with red wine
Bouchée	Small pastry case
Bouillabaisse	Fish stew with garlic
Bourguignonne	Cooked in Burgundy wine and onion
Brochette	Meat or fish grilled on a skewer
Café complet	Coffee with rolls or bread and jam
Canapé	Toast or biscuit with savoury topping
Caneton	Duckling
Canneloni	Pasta tubes stuffed with meat in sauce
Carbonnade	Meat casserole with beer
Champignons	Mushrooms
Chasseur	Cooked with shallots, mushrooms and white wine
Châteaubriand	Double fillet steak
Compôte	Stewed fruit
Consommé	Clear soup
Crêpes Suzettes	Thin pancakes in flaming orange liqueur sauce
Croûte	Large round of toast used as a base
Croûtons	Small cubes of fried bread or toasted bread
Demi-tasse	Small coffee cup
Devilled	Served with sharp hot seasoning

Dindonneau	Young turkey
Entrecôte	Sirloin Steak
Escalope	Thin slice of meat (usually veal)
Escargots	Snails
Espagnole	Spanish style
Filet	Boneless cut of meat or fish
Flambé	Served with flaming liqueur
Framboise	Raspberry
Fricassé	White stew of chicken or veal
Fromage	Cheese
Fumé	Smoked
Gibier	Game
Gnocchi	Poached dumplings
Goujons	small strips of white fish
Goulash	Spiced meat stew with potato
Grecque	Greek style
Haricot	Meat stew with vegetables
Haricots verts	French beans
Hollandaise sauce	A rich butter and egg sauce with lemon juice
Homard	Lobster
Hors d'oeuvres	Small appetisers
Huitres	Oysters
Jambon	Ham
Jardinière	With fresh spring vegetables
Juliènne	Fine strips of mixed vegetables
Kebab	Cubes of meat and vegetables cooked on a skewer
Langue	Tongue
Lasagne	Flat pasta noodles
Legumes	Vegetables
Longe	Loin of meat
Lyonnaise	With onions
Macedoine	Mixed fruit or vegetables cut in even dice
Mais	Sweetcorn
Maquereau	Mackerel
Marrons	Chestnut
Médaillon	Small rounds of meat, fish or pate
Meunière	Usually fish, lightly fried in butter with lemon juice
Mocha	Blend of chocolate and coffee
Mornay	White sauce with cheese
Moule	Mussel
Mousse	Light whipped cream sweet or savoury
Navarin	Stew of mutton or lamb with vegetables
Noisette	Boneless round or oval cut of lamb, veal or beef
Nouilles	Noodles
Oeufs	Eggs
Oie	Goose

Paella	Meat, seafood and vegetables pan fried with rice
Pain	Bread
Pamplemousse	Grapefruit
Parfait	Rich ice cream with cream and fruit
Parmentier	With potatoes
Paté	A smooth or rough savoury paste
Paupiettes	Slices of meat or fish folded and stuffed
Petit fours	Very small fancy marzipan cakes and fruits
Pilaf	Savoury rice
Plat du jour	Dish of the day
Pomme	Apple or potato
Potage	Thick soup
Poulet	Chicken
Profiterole	Small light pastry ball
Provençale	With garlic and tomato
Quenelles	Light meat, fish or poultry dumpling in sauce
Quiche	Savoury tartlet or pie
Ragout	Meat or fish stew
Ramequin	Cheese tartlet
Ratatouille	Vegetable stew
Ratafia	Macaroon biscuit
Ravioli	Pasta square stuffed with meat in sauce
Risotto	Savoury rice
Roulade	Stuffed meat roll
Sabayon	Rich dessert with eggs, cream and wine
Salmis	Game stew
Savarin	Sponge ring
Sorbet	Water ice
Soufflé	Light frothy sweet or savoury egg dish
Table d'hôte	Complete meal with limited choice at an inclusive price
Tartare sauce	Mayonnaise with chopped herbs
Tournedos	Small round trimmed fillet steak
Truffle	Rare black mushroom
Truite	Trout
Vacherin	Meringue nest
Vichysoisse	Leek and potato soup with chopped chives (serve hot or cold)
Volaille	Poultry
Vol-au-vent	Hollow puff pastry case

Index